Flask Blueprints

Dive into the world of the Flask microframework to
develop an array of web applications

Joël Perras

PUBLISHING

BIRMINGHAM - MUMBAI

Flask Blueprints

First published: November 2015

Production reference: 1251115

Published by Packt Publishing Ltd.
Livery Place
35 Livery Street
Birmingham B3 2PB, UK.

ISBN 978-1-78439-478-3

www.packtpub.com

Credits

Author
Joël Perras

Reviewers
Shalabh Aggarwal

Christoph Heer

Andreas Porevopoulos

Commissioning Editor
Julian Ursell

Acquisition Editor
Meeta Rajani

Content Development Editor
Shweta Pant

Technical Editor
Bharat Patil

Copy Editor
Tasneem Fatehi

Project Coordinator
Sanjeet Rao

Proofreader
Safis Editing

Indexer
Monica Ajmera Mehta

Graphics
Disha Haria

Production Coordinator
Nilesh R. Mohite

Cover Work
Nilesh R. Mohite

About the Author

Joël Perras has been professionally involved in technology and computing for over 12 years. He got his start in the world of programming by attempting to teach himself Java at the tender age of 13 and got his first job at a small web development firm a few years later writing Java Server Pages. The first site he built is still running.

While studying physics and mathematics at McGill University in Montréal, he helped set up a Tier II analysis centre for the Worldwide LHC Computing Grid, which cemented his interest in distributed systems architecture and high performance computing.

Currently, his days are spent building infrastructure and Python applications with the incredible people at Fictive Kin, writing open source code, and trying to lift heavy weights over his head on a regular basis.

I'd like to thank Sara for her infinite patience throughout the process of writing this lengthy technical manual and my coworkers at Fictive Kin for dealing with my particularly bad sense of humor on a daily basis.

About the Reviewers

Shalabh Aggarwal has several years of experience in developing business systems and web applications for small-to-medium scale industries. He started his career working on Python, and although he works on multiple technologies, he remains a Python developer at heart. He is passionate about open source technologies and writes highly readable and quality code.

Shalabh is also active in voluntary training for engineering students on nonconventional and open source topics. When not working with full-time assignments, he acts as a consultant for start-ups on leveraging different technologies. He is pursuing his master's degree in business from IIT Delhi.

> I would like to thank my family, my mother, and my sister for putting up with me during my long writing and research sessions. I would also like to thank my friends and colleagues who encouraged me and kept the momentum going. I would like to thank Armin Ronacher for developing this wonderful web framework.

Christoph Heer is a passionate Python developer based in Germany. He likes to develop web applications and also tools and systems for infrastructure optimization, management, and monitoring. He is proud to be a part of the great Python community and wishes to have more time for open source contribution.

Andreas Porevopoulos has loved computers and programming since he was in high school and over the years he has developed many apps in different languages and systems, but Python was always his favorite. He has been working as a Full Stack Python developer for the last 7 years and has completed lots of projects in Django and Flask. He believes that these two frameworks are among the best for web app development.

The agile practices that he uses for all his developing/deploying needs are Git, Ansible, Vagrant, and Docker.

www.PacktPub.com

Support files, eBooks, discount offers, and more

For support files and downloads related to your book, please visit www.PacktPub.com.

Did you know that Packt offers eBook versions of every book published, with PDF and ePub files available? You can upgrade to the eBook version at www.PacktPub.com and as a print book customer, you are entitled to a discount on the eBook copy. Get in touch with us at service@packtpub.com for more details.

At www.PacktPub.com, you can also read a collection of free technical articles, sign up for a range of free newsletters and receive exclusive discounts and offers on Packt books and eBooks.

https://www2.packtpub.com/books/subscription/packtlib

Do you need instant solutions to your IT questions? PacktLib is Packt's online digital book library. Here, you can search, access, and read Packt's entire library of books.

Why subscribe?

- Fully searchable across every book published by Packt
- Copy and paste, print, and bookmark content
- On demand and accessible via a web browser

Free access for Packt account holders

If you have an account with Packt at www.PacktPub.com, you can use this to access PacktLib today and view 9 entirely free books. Simply use your login credentials for immediate access.

Table of Contents

Preface

The setting is familiar enough: you're a web developer who has worked with a few programming languages, frameworks and environments, and decided to learn enough Python to make a few toy web applications. Maybe you've already used some Python web frameworks to build an application or two, and want to explore a few of the alternative options that you keep hearing about.

This is usually how people come to know about Flask.

As a microframework, Flask is built to help you and then get out of your way. Taking a very different approach from most other general-purpose web frameworks, Flask consists of a very small core that handles the processing and normalization of HTTP and the WSGI specification (via Werkzeug) and provides an exceptionally good templating language (via Jinja2). The beauty of Flask lies in its intrinsic extensibility: as it was designed from the start to do very little, it was also designed to be extended very easily. A pleasant consequence of this is that you are not beholden to a particular database abstraction layer, authentication protocol, or caching mechanism.

Learning a new framework is not simply about learning the basic functions and objects that are provided to you: it's often as important to learn how the framework can be adapted to help you build the specific requirements of your application.

This book will demonstrate how to develop a series of web application projects with the Python web microframework, and leverage extensions and external Python libraries/APIs to extend the development of a variety of larger and more complex web applications.

What this book covers

Chapter 1, Starting on the Right Foot – Using Virtualenv, kicks off our dive into Python web application development with the basics of using and managing virtual environments to isolate the application dependencies. We will look at the setup tools, pip, libraries, and utilities that are used to install and distribute reusable packages of Python code, and virtualenv, a tool to create isolated environments for the Python-based software requirements of a project. We will also discuss what these tools are not able to do, and look at the virtualenvwrapper abstraction to augment the functionality that virtualenv provides.

Chapter 2, Small to Big – Growing the Flask Application Structure, explores the various baseline layouts and configurations that you might consider for a Flask application. The pros and cons of each approach are outlined as we progress from the simplest one-file application structure to the more complex, multipackage Blueprint architecture.

Chapter 3, Snap – the Code Snippet Sharing Application, builds our first simple Flask application centered around learning the basics of one of the most popular relational database abstractions, SQLAlchemy, and several of the most popular Flask extensions: Flask-Login to handle authenticated user login sessions, Flask-Bcrypt to ensure that account passwords are stored in a secure manner, and Flask-WTF to create and process form-based input data.

Chapter 4, Socializer – the Testable Timeline, builds a very simple data model for a social web application where the main focus is on unit and functional testing using pytest, the Python testing framework and tools. We will also explore the use of the application factory pattern, which allows us to instantiate separate versions of our application for the purposes of simplifying testing. Additionally, the use and creation of often-omitted (and forgotten) signals, provided by the Blinker library, are described in detail.

Chapter 5, Shutterbug, the Photo Stream API, builds a skeleton of an application around a JSON-based API, which is a requirement for any modern web application these days. One of the many API-based Flask extensions, Flask-RESTful, is used to prototype the API, where we also delve into simple authentication mechanisms for stateless systems and even write a few tests along the way. A short detour is made into the world of Werkzeug, the WSGI toolkit that Flask is built upon, to build a custom WSGI middleware that allows the seamless handling of URI-based version numbers for our nascent API.

Chapter 6, Hublot – Flask CLI Tools, covers a topic that is often omitted from most web application framework discussions: command-line tools. The use of Flask-Script is explained, and several CLI-based tools are created to interact with the data models of our application. Additionally, we will build our very own custom Flask extension that wraps an existing Python library to fetch the repository and issue information from the GitHub API.

Chapter 7, Dinnerly – Recipe Sharing, introduces the somewhat intimidating concept of the OAuth authorization flow that many large web applications, such as Twitter, Facebook, and GitHub, implement in order to allow third-party applications to act on behalf of the account owners without compromising basic account security credentials. A barebones data model is constructed for a recipe-sharing application that allows the so-called social sign in and the ability to cross-post the data from our application to the feeds or streams of the services that a user has connected. Finally, we will introduce the concept of database migrations using Alembic, which allow you to synchronize your SQLAlchemy model metadata with the schemas of the underlying relational database tables in a reliable manner.

What you need for this book

To work through most of the examples in this book, all you need is your favorite text editor or IDE, access to the Internet (to install the various Flask extensions, not to mention Flask itself), a relational database (one of SQLite, MySQL, or PostgreSQL), a browser, and some familiarity with the command line. Care has been taken to indicate when additional packages or libraries are required to complete the examples in each chapter.

Who this book is for

This book was created for the new Python developers who wish to dive into the world of web application development, or for the seasoned Python web application professional who is interested in learning about Flask and the extension-based ecosystem behind it. To get the most out of each chapter, you should have a solid understanding of the Python programming language, a basic knowledge of relational database systems, and fluency with the command line.

Conventions

In this book, you will find a number of styles of text that distinguish between different kinds of information. Here are some examples of these styles, and an explanation of their meaning.

Code words in text, database table names, folder names, filenames, file extensions, pathnames, dummy URLs, user input, and Twitter handles are shown as follows: "This will create a blank `app1` environment and activate it. You should see an (app1) tag in your shell prompt."

A block of code is set as follows:

```
[default]
  <div>{{ form.password.label }}: {{ form.password }}</div>
  {% if form.password.errors %}
  <ul class="errors">{% for error in form.password.errors %}<li>{{
error }}</li>{% endfor %}</ul>
  {% endif %}

  <div><input type="submit" value="Sign up!"></div>
</form>

{% endblock %}
```

When we wish to draw your attention to a particular part of a code block, the relevant lines or items are set in bold:

```
from application.users.views import users
app.register_blueprint(users, url_prefix='/users')

from application.posts.views import posts
app.register_blueprint(posts, url_prefix='/posts')

    # ...
```

Any command-line input or output is written as follows:

```
$ source ~/envs/testing/bin/activate
(testing)$ pip uninstall numpy
```

New terms and **important words** are shown in bold. Words that you see on the screen, in menus or dialog boxes for example, appear in the text like this: "Then it asserts that the **Sign up!** button text appears in the returned HTML".

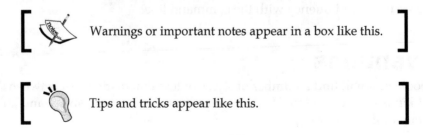

Warnings or important notes appear in a box like this.

Tips and tricks appear like this.

Reader feedback

Feedback from our readers is always welcome. Let us know what you think about this book—what you liked or may have disliked. Reader feedback is important for us to develop titles that you really get the most out of.

To send us general feedback, simply send an e-mail to feedback@packtpub.com, and mention the book title via the subject of your message.

If there is a topic that you have expertise in and you are interested in either writing or contributing to a book, see our author guide on www.packtpub.com/authors.

Customer support

Now that you are the proud owner of a Packt book, we have a number of things to help you to get the most from your purchase.

Downloading the example code

You can download the example code files for all Packt books you have purchased from your account at http://www.packtpub.com. If you purchased this book elsewhere, you can visit http://www.packtpub.com/support and register to have the files e-mailed directly to you.

Errata

Although we have taken every care to ensure the accuracy of our content, mistakes do happen. If you find a mistake in one of our books—maybe a mistake in the text or the code—we would be grateful if you would report this to us. By doing so, you can save other readers from frustration and help us improve subsequent versions of this book. If you find any errata, please report them by visiting http://www.packtpub.com/submit-errata, selecting your book, clicking on the **errata submission form** link, and entering the details of your errata. Once your errata are verified, your submission will be accepted and the errata will be uploaded on our website, or added to any list of existing errata, under the Errata section of that title. Any existing errata can be viewed by selecting your title from http://www.packtpub.com/support.

Piracy

Piracy of copyright material on the Internet is an ongoing problem across all media. At Packt, we take the protection of our copyright and licenses very seriously. If you come across any illegal copies of our works, in any form, on the Internet, please provide us with the location address or website name immediately so that we can pursue a remedy.

Please contact us at copyright@packtpub.com with a link to the suspected pirated material.

We appreciate your help in protecting our authors, and our ability to bring you valuable content.

Questions

You can contact us at questions@packtpub.com if you are having a problem with any aspect of the book, and we will do our best to address it.

1
Starting on the Right Foot – Using Virtualenv

One of the great difficulties in modern software development is that of dependency management. Generally, a dependency of a software project consists of a library or component that is required for the project to function correctly. In the case of a Flask application (and more generally, that of a Python application), most dependencies are comprised of specially organized and annotated source files. Once created, these packages of source files may then be included in other projects and so forth. For some, this chain of dependencies can become an unmanageable mess, where the slightest alteration to any of the libraries in the chain can cause a cascade of incompatibilities that would bring further development to a screeching halt. In the Python world, as you may know already, the fundamental unit of a reusable set of source files is that of a Python module (a file that contains definitions and statements). Once you've created a module on your local filesystem and ensured that it is in your system's PYTHONPATH, including it in a newly created project is as simple as specifying the import, which is as follows:

```
import the_custom_module
```

Where the_custom_module.py is a file that exists somewhere in $PYTHONPATH of the system executing the program.

> The $PYTHONPATH can include paths to the compressed archives (.zip folders) in addition to the normal file paths.

This is not where the story ends, of course. While modules littering your local filesystem might be convenient at first, what happens when you want to share some of the code that you've written for others? Usually, this would entail emailing/ Dropboxing the files in question, however, this is obviously a very cumbersome and error-prone solution. Thankfully, this is a problem that has been considered and some progress has been made in alleviating the common issues. The most significant of these advances is the subject of this chapter, and how the following techniques for creating reusable, isolated packages of code can be leveraged to ease the development of a Flask application:

- Python packaging with pip and setuptools
- Encapsulation of virtual environments with virtualenv

The solution presented by the various Python packaging paradigms/libraries is far from perfect; one sure way to start an argument with a passionate Python developer is to proclaim that the *packaging problem* has been solved! We still have a long way to go for that but headway is being made in incremental steps with improvements to setuptools and various other libraries used in building, maintaining, and distributing a reusable Python code.

In this chapter, when we refer to a package, what we will actually be talking about would be succinctly described as a distribution — a bundle of software to be installed from a remote source — and not a collection of modules in a folder structure that utilizes the `__init__.py` convention in order to delineate the folders containing the modules that we want to be importable.

Setuptools and pip

When a developer wants to make their code more widely available, one of the first steps will be to create a setuptools-compatible package.

Most of the distributions of a modern Python version will come with setuptools already installed. If it is not present on your system of choice, then obtaining it is relatively simple, with additional instructions available on the official documentation:

```
wget https://bootstrap.pypa.io/ez_setup.py -O - | python
```

After setuptools is installed, the basic requirement to create a compatible package is the creation of a `setup.py` file at the root of your project. The primary content of this file should be the invocation of a `setup()` function with a few mandatory (and many optional) arguments, as follows:

```
from setuptools import setup
```

```
setup(
    name="My Great Project",
    version="0.0.1",
    author="Jane Doe",
    author_email="jane@example.com",
    description= "A brief summary of the project.",
    license="BSD",
    keywords="example tutorial flask",
    url="http://example.com/my-great-project",
    packages=['foobar','tests'],
    long_description="A much longer project description.",
    classifiers=[
        "Development Status :: 3 - Alpha",
        "Topic :: Utilities",
        "License :: OSI Approved :: BSD License",
    ],
)
```

Downloading the example code

You can download the example code files from your account at `http://www.packtpub.com` for all the Packt Publishing books you have purchased. If you purchased this book elsewhere, you can visit `http://www.packtpub.com/support` and register to have the files e-mailed directly to you.

Once the package has been created, most developers will choose to upload their newly minted package to PyPI—the official source of nearly all Python packages—using the built-in tools that are provided by setuptools itself. While the use of this particular public PyPI repository is not a requirement (it's even possible to set up your own personal package index), most Python developers will expect to find their packages here.

This brings us to one more essential piece of the puzzle—the `pip` Python package installer. If you have Python 2.7.9 or greater installed, then `pip` will already be present. Some distributions might have it preinstalled for you or it might be present in a system-level package. For a Debian-like distribution of Linux, it may be installed via the following command:

```
apt-get install python-pip
```

Similarly, other Linux-based distributions will have their own recommended package managers. If you'd rather obtain the source and install it manually, it is a simple matter of fetching a file and running it using the Python interpreter:

```
$ curl -o get-pip.py https://bootstrap.pypa.io/get-pip.py
$ python get-pip.py
```

Pip is a tool for installing Python packages (and is itself a Python package). While it is not the only player in the game, `pip` is by far the most widely used.

> The predecessor to `pip` is `easy_install`, which has largely been replaced in the Python community by the former. The `easy_install` module suffered some relatively major problems, such as allowing partially completed installations, the inability to uninstall a package without requiring the user to manually delete the related `.egg` files, and console output that contained the useful success and error messages that allowed the developer to determine the best course of action in case something went wrong.

One can invoke pip in the command line to install, say, a scientific computing package on the local filesystem:

```
$ pip install numpy
```

The preceding command will query the default PyPI index for a package named numpy and download the latest version to a special place in your system, usually `/usr/local/lib/pythonX.Y/site-packages` (X and Y are the major/minor versions of the Python version that `pip` points to). This operation may require root privileges and would thus require `sudo` or similar actions to allow it to be completed.

One of the many benefits of virtual environments, which we will explore shortly, is that they generally avoid the privilege escalation requirement that can plague system-level changes to installed packages.

Once this operation is completed successfully, you now have the ability to import the numpy package into new modules and use any and all of the functionalities that it exposes:

```
import numpy

x = numpy.array([1, 2, 3])
sum = numpy.sum(x)
print sum  # prints 6
```

Once we have this package (or any other, for that matter) installed, there's nothing stopping us from fetching additional packages in the usual way. Moreover, we can install multiple packages at the same time by providing their names as additional arguments to the `install` command:

```
$ pip install scipy pandas # etc.
```

Avoiding dependency hell, the Python way

New developers might be tempted to install every interesting package that they come across. In doing so, they might realize that this quickly degrades into a Kafkaesque situation where previously installed packages may cease to function and newly installed packages may behave unpredictably, if they manage to get installed successfully at all. The problem with the preceding approach, as some of you may have guessed, is that of conflicting package dependencies. Say for example, we have package A installed; it depends on version 1 of package Q and version 1 of package R. Package B depends on version 2 of package R (where versions 1 and 2 are not API-compatible). Pip will happily install package B for you, which will upgrade package R to version 2. This will, at best, make package A completely unusable or, at worst, make it behave in undocumented and unpredictable ways.

The Python ecosystem has come up with a solution to the basic issues that arise from what is colloquially referred to as **dependency hell**. While far from perfect, it allows developers to sidestep many of the simplest package version dependency conflicts that can arise in web application development.

The `virtualenv` tool, of which a similar implementation is now a default module in Python 3.3 and named `venv`, is essential to ensure that you minimize your chances of ending up in dependency hell. The following quote is from the introduction in the official documentation for `virtualenv`:

> *It creates an environment that has its own installation directories, that doesn't share libraries with other virtualenv environments (and optionally doesn't access the globally installed libraries either).*

More concisely, `virtualenv` allows you to create isolated environments for each one of your Python applications (or any Python code).

 The `virtualenv` tool does not, however, help you to manage the dependencies of the Python C-based extensions. For example, if you install the `lxml` package from `pip`, it will require that you have the correct `libxml2` and `libxslt` system libraries and headers (which it will link against). The `virtualenv` tool will not help you isolate these system-level libraries.

Working with virtualenv

First, we need to make sure that we have the `virtualenv` tool installed in our local system. This is a simple matter of fetching it from the PyPI repository:

```
$ pip install virtualenv
```

 For obvious reasons, this package should be installed outside any virtual environments that may already exist.

Creating a new virtual environment

Creating a new virtual environment is straightforward. The following command will create a new folder at the specified path that will contain the necessary structure and scripts, including a full copy of your default Python binary:

```
$ virtualenv <path/to/env/directory>
```

If we want to create an environment that lives at `~/envs/testing`, we will first ensure that the parent directory exists and then invoke the following command:

```
$ mkdir -p ~/envs
$ virtualenv ~/envs/testing
```

In Python 3.3+, a mostly API-compatible version of the `virtualenv` tool was added to the default language packages. The name of the module is `venv`, however, the name of the script that allows you to create a virtual environment is `pyvenv` and can be invoked in a similar way as the previously discussed `virtualenv` tool, as follows:

```
$ mkdir -p ~/envs
$ pyvenv ~/envs/testing
```

Activating and deactivating virtual environments

Creating a virtual environment does not automatically activate it. Once the environment is created, we need to activate it so that any modifications to the Python environment (for example, installing packages) will occur in the isolated environment instead of our system global one. By default, the activation of a virtual environment will alter the prompt string ($PS1) of the currently active user so that it displays the name of the sourced virtual environment:

```
$ source ~/envs/testing/bin/activate
(testing) $ # Command prompt modified to display current virtualenv
```

The command is the same for Python 3.3+:

```
$ source ~/envs/testing/bin/activate
(testing) $ # Command prompt modified to display current virtualenv
```

When you run the above command, the following series of steps occurs:

1. Deactivates any already activated environment.
2. Prepends your $PATH variable with the location of the virtualenv bin/ directory, for example, ~/envs/testing/bin:$PATH.
3. Unsets $PYTHONHOME if it exists.
4. Modifies your interactive shell prompt so that it includes the name of the currently active virtualenv.

As a result of the $PATH environment variable manipulations, the Python and pip binaries (and whatever other binaries that were installed via pip), which have been invoked via the shell where the environment was activated, will be the ones contained in ~/envs/testing/bin.

Adding packages to an existing environment

We can easily add packages to a virtual environment by simply activating it and then invoking pip in the following way:

```
$ source ~/envs/testing/bin/activate
(testing)$ pip install numpy
```

This will install the numpy package to the testing environment, and only the testing environment. Your global system packages will be unaffected, as well as any other existing environments.

Uninstalling packages from an existing environment

Uninstalling a `pip` package is straightforward as well:

```
$ source ~/envs/testing/bin/activate
(testing)$ pip uninstall numpy
```

This will remove the `numpy` package from the testing environment only.

Here is one relatively major place where the Python package management falls short: uninstalling a package does not uninstall its dependencies. For example, if you install package A and it installs dependent packages B and C, uninstalling package A at a later time will not uninstall B and C.

Simplifying common operations – using the virtualenvwrapper tool

A tool that I use frequently is `virtualenvwrapper`, which is a very small set of smart defaults and command aliases that makes working with virtual environments more intuitive. Let's install this to our global system now:

```
$ pip install virtualenvwrapper
```

 This will also install the `virtualenv` package as well in case it is not already present.

Next, you'll want to add the following lines to the end of your shell startup file. This is most likely `~/.bashrc`, but in case you've changed your default shell to something else such as `zsh`, then it could be different (for example, `~/.zshrc`):

```
export WORKON_HOME=$HOME/.virtualenvs
source /usr/local/bin/virtualenvwrapper.sh
```

The first line in the preceding code block indicates that new virtual environments that are created with `virtualenvwrapper` should be stored in `$HOME/.virtualenvs`. You can modify this as you see fit, but I generally leave this as a good default. I find that keeping all my virtual environments in the same hidden folder in my home directory reduces the amount of clutter in individual projects and makes it a bit more difficult to mistakenly add a whole virtual environment to version control.

Adding an entire virtual environment to version control might seem like a good idea, but things are never as simple as they seem. The moment someone running a slightly (or completely) different operating system decides to download your project, which includes a full `virtualenv` folder that may contain packages with `C` modules that were compiled against your own architecture, they're going to have a hard time getting things to work.

Instead, a common pattern that is supported by pip and used by many developers is to freeze the current state of the installed packages in a virtual environment and save this to a `requirements.txt` file:

```
(testing) $ pip freeze > requirements.txt
```

This file may then be added to a **version control system** (**VCS**). As the intent of the file is to declare which dependencies are required for the application, and not provide them or indicate how they should be constructed, users of your project are then free to obtain the required packages in any way they so choose. Generally, they will install them via `pip`, which can handle a requirements file just fine:

```
(testing) $ pip install -r  requirements.txt
```

The second line adds a few convenient aliases to your current shell environment in order to create, activate, switch, and remove environments:

- `mkvirtualenv test`: This will create an environment named test and activate it automatically.

- `mktmpenv test`: This will create a temporary environment named test and activate it automatically. This environment will be destroyed once you invoke the deactivate script.

- `workon app`: This will switch you to the app environment (already created).

- `workon` (alias `lsvirtualenv`): When you don't specify an environment, this will print all the existing environments that are available.

- `deactivate`: This will disable the currently active environment, if any.

- `rmvirtualenv app`: This will completely remove the app environment.

We'll use the following command to create an environment to install our application packages:

```
$ mkvirtualenv app1
```

This will create a blank app1 environment and activate it. You should see an (app1) tag in your shell prompt.

> If you are using a shell other than Bash or ZSH, this environment tag may or may not appear. The way in which this works is that the script that is used to activate the virtual environment also modifies your current prompt string (the PS1 environment variable) so that it indicates the currently active virtualenv. As a result, there is a chance that this may not work if you're using a very special or non-standard shell configuration.

Summary

In this chapter, we looked at one of the most fundamental problems that any non-trivial Python application faces: library dependency management. Thankfully, the Python ecosystem has developed the widely adopted virtualenv tool for solving the most common subset of dependency problems that developers may encounter.

Additionally, we looked at a tool, virtualenvwrapper, that abstracted away some of the most common operations that one would perform with virtualenv. While we listed some of the functionalities that this package provided, the list of things that virtualenvwrapper can do is much more extensive. We only presented the very basics here, but more in-depth learning about what this tool can do is indispensable if you work with Python virtual environments all day long.

2
Small to Big – Growing the Flask Application Structure

Flask is a wonderful framework for people who want to write a very quick single-file application in order to prototype an API or to build a drop-dead simple website. What isn't immediately obvious, however, is just how flexible and adept Flask is at growing in larger, more modular application structures that are a necessity once the single-module layout becomes more burdensome than convenient. The major points that we will cover in this chapter are as follows:

- How to convert a module-based Flask application to a package-based layout
- How to implement Flask blueprints on top of a package-based application structure
- How to ensure that our resulting application can be run with the built-in Werkzeug development server

Your first Flask application structure

The canonical Flask introductory application that is found on the official website is a paragon of simplicity, and is something you've most likely come across beforehand:

```
# app.py
from flask import Flask
app = Flask(__name__)


@app.route("/")
def hello():
```

```
    return "Hello World!"


if __name__ == "__main__":
app.run()
```

The preceding application can be run by first installing the `Flask` package from `pip` (all in a virtual environment, of course) and then executing the script itself under the Python interpreter:

```
$ pip install Flask
$ python app.py
```

This will start the Werkzeug development web server, which was installed when `Flask` was obtained via `pip`, and serve the application on `http://localhost:5000` by default.

The typical way in which people start a new `Flask` application is to add various endpoints to the incredibly simple module that we showed in the preceding section:

```
from flask import Flask, request
app = Flask(__name__)



@app.route("/")
def hello():
    return "Hello World!"



@app.route("/contact")
def contact():
    return "You can contact me at 555-5555, or "
    " email me at test@example.com"



@app.route('/login', methods=['GET', 'POST'])
def login():
    if request.method == 'POST':
        # Logic for handling login
        pass
    else:
```

```
        # Display login form
        pass


if __name__ == "__main__":
    app.run()
```

While straightforward, the drawbacks of this approach become apparent once the complexity of the application increases:

- The number of function definitions in the module increases almost linearly with the number of URLs that we want to route to. Though this is not an intrinsic drawback, developers should prefer to split functionality into smaller packages that are easier to understand.

- The templates and static files that are required by the routes accumulate in the same sub-folder location, thus making their organization more complex and error-prone.

- Certain operations (for example, logging) become simpler when they are configured on a per-package basis instead of in one monolithic module.

From module to package

The simplest structural change that can be applied to a module-based Flask application is to transform it into a typical Python package, with special accommodation for the static and templates folders.

```
application
└──application
        ├──__init__.py
        ├──static
        │     ├──app.js
        │     └──styles.css
        └──templates
              ├──index.html
              └──layout.html
```

Here, we created a top-level application package, moved the app.py module along with the static and template folders inside it, and renamed it __init__.py.

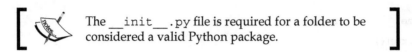 The __init__.py file is required for a folder to be considered a valid Python package.

One detail that should be handled at this point is the code that is used to run the development server. If you recall, the single-module application contained the following conditional statement:

```
if __name__ == "__main__":
    app.run()
```

This allows us to execute the module file with the Python interpreter directly, as follows:

```
$ python app.py
* Running on http://localhost:5000/
```

For a variety of reasons, this is no longer a viable option. However, we still wish to run the development server in a straightforward fashion. For this, we will create a run.py file as a sibling to the inner application package folder:

```
├─application
│   ├─__init__.py
│   ├─static
│   │   ├─app.js
│   │   └─styles.css
│   └─templates
│       ├─index.html
│       └─layout.html
└─run.py
```

In the run.py file, we will add the following snippet:

```
from application import app
app.run()
```

This allows us to invoke the following command via the CLI so as to run the development server in the usual way:

```
$ python run.py
```

Generally, it's considered as bad practice to include code that modifies a state (for example, the creation of the Flask app object) in a __init__.py package. We do this now only for illustrative purposes.

The `run` method of our Flask application object can accept a few optional arguments. The following are the most useful ones:

- `host`: The host IP to bind to. Defaults to any port, which is denoted by `0.0.0.0`.
- `port`: The port the application will bind to. Defaults to `5000`.
- `debug`: If set to `True`, the Werkzeug development server will reload when it detects a code change and additionally provide an interactive debugger embedded in an HTML page when an unhandled exception occurs.

With the new application structure that we've outlined in the preceding section, it's relatively simple to see how functionality such as route handler definitions, can be split from __init__.py into something like a `views.py` module. Similarly, our data models can be factored into a `models.py` module, as follows:

```
application

├──application

|    ├──__init__.py

|    ├──models.py

|    ├──static

|    |    ├──app.js

|    |    └──styles.css

|    ├──templates

|    |    ├──index.html

|    |    └──layout.html

|    └──views.py

└──run.py
```

We simply need to import these modules in __init__.py in order to ensure that they are loaded when we run the application:

```
from flask import Flask
app = Flask(__name__)


import application.models
import application.views
```

 Note that we need to import the views after we instantiate the application object, otherwise a circular import will be created. Once we start developing applications with blueprints, we will generally try to avoid circular imports by ensuring that one blueprint does not import from another.

Similarly, we must import the Flask application object to the views.py module so that we can use the @app.route decorator to define our route handlers:

```
from application import app


@app.route("/")
def hello():
    return "Hello World!"



@app.route("/contact")
def contact():
    return "You can contact me at 555-5555, or "
    " email me at test@example.com"



@app.route('/login', methods=['GET', 'POST'])
def login():
    if request.method == 'POST':
        # Logic for handling login
        pass
    else:
        # Display login form
        pass
```

As expected, the application can still be run using the built-in Werkzeug application server from the **command-line interface (CLI)** as before; the only thiwng that has changed is the organization of our files. The advantage that we gained (at the cost of additional files and the possibility of circular imports rearing their ugly heads) is that of functional separation and organization: our view handlers may be grouped together in single or multiple modules based on their domain of interest, and our data layer and utility functions may exist elsewhere in the application structure.

From package to blueprint

The package-based application structure that we just explored may be suitable for a large number of applications. However, Flask offers us a level of abstraction **née Blueprints**, which formalizes and enforces a separation of concerns at the level of views.

 Do not confuse the concept of a blueprint in Flask, which is an abstraction to factor an application into more discrete components, with that of the Packt book series by the same name!

A Flask application that has become too unwieldy can be factored into a set of discrete blueprints—each with their own mapping of URIs and view functions, static resources (for example, JavaScript and CSS files), Jinja templates, and even Flask extensions. In many respects, blueprints are very similar to the Flask applications themselves. However, a blueprint is not an independent Flask application and cannot be run independently as an application itself, as described in the official Flask documentation:

> *A blueprint in Flask is not a pluggable app because it is not actually an application – it's a set of operations which can be registered on an application, even multiple times. – Official Flask documentation,* `http://flask.pocoo.org/docs/0.10/blueprints/`

As a result, all the blueprints in an application will share the same main application object and configuration, and they must be registered with the main Flask object before the URI dispatching can occur.

Our first blueprint

The previous package-based application layout can be extended to include a blueprint-based architecture by first adding a new package that will contain our blueprint, which we will simply call users:

```
├──application
|   ├── __init__.py
|   └──users
|   ├── __init__.py
|   └──views.py
└──run.py
```

The contents of the users package consists of the requisite __init__.py and one other module, views.py. Our (simple, for now) view functions for the users blueprint will be placed in the views.py module:

```python
from flask import Blueprint


users = Blueprint('users', __name__)



@users.route('/me')
def me():
    return "This is my page.", 200
```

We could have placed this code in the users/__init__.py file instead of separating it out into its own views.py module; but in doing so, we would be placing a side effect-generating code (that is, the instantiation of the users Blueprint object) in package initialization, which is generally frowned upon. The minor additional complexity of separating it out into a different module will save you from headaches later on.

In this new module, we imported the Blueprint class from Flask and used it to instantiate a users blueprint object. The Blueprint class has two required arguments, name and import_name, which we provide as users and the __name__ global magic attribute available to all Python modules and scripts. The former may be any unique identifier among all the registered blueprints that we desire and the latter should be the name of the module where the blueprint object is instantiated.

Once we have this in place, we must amend our application initialization in `application/__init__.py` in order to bind the blueprint to the Flask application object:

```
from flask import Flask
from application.users.views import users


app = Flask(__name__)
app.register_blueprint(users, url_prefix='/users')
```

On registering the Blueprint object with the application instance, there are several optional arguments that can be specified. One of these arguments is `url_prefix`, which will automatically prefix all the routes defined in the blueprint in question with the given string. This makes it quite simple to encapsulate all the views and routes that are meant to process the requests for any endpoints that begin with the `/users/*` URI segment, and is a pattern we will use frequently throughout this book.

Once completed, we can run our application using the built-in Werkzeug application server in the usual way via our `run.py` script:

```
$ python run.py
```

Opening up our browser of choice and navigating to `http://localhost:5000/users/me` yields the following rendered result:

Summary

In this chapter, we started out with the most common, simple Flask application architecture and explored a few of the ways in which we can extend it in order to allow for a more modular approach. We first went from a module-based layout to a package-based one and then graduated to the use of Flask blueprints, which paved the way for the basic application structure that we will use in the following chapters.

In the next chapter, we will use the knowledge that we gained here to create our first functional Flask application by utilizing the blueprint pattern and several well-known Flask extensions.

3
Snap – the Code Snippet Sharing Application

In this chapter, we will build our first fully functional, database-backed application. This application, codenamed Snap, will allow users to create an account with a username and password. Users will be allowed to login, logout, add and list the so-called semiprivate *snaps* of text that can be shared with others.

For this chapter, you should be familiar with at least one of the following relational database systems: PostgreSQL, MySQL, or SQLite. Additionally, some knowledge of the SQLAlchemy Python library, which acts as an abstraction layer and object-relational mapper for these (and several other) databases, will be an asset. If you are not well versed in the usage of SQLAlchemy, fear not. We will have a gentle introduction to the library that will bring new developers up to speed and serve as a refresher for the more experienced.

From this point on, in the book, the SQLite database will be our relational database of choice. The other database systems that we listed are all client/server-based with a multitude of configuration options that may need adjustment depending on the system they are installed in, while SQLite's default mode of operation is self-contained, serverless, and zero-configuration.

We suggest that you use SQLite to work with this project and the projects in the following chapters, but any major relational database supported by SQLAlchemy will do.

Getting started

To make sure we start things correctly, let's create a folder where this project will exist and a virtual environment to encapsulate any dependencies that we will require:

```
$ mkdir -p ~/src/snap && cd ~/src/snap
$ mkvirtualenv snap -i flask
```

This will create a folder called `snap` at the given path and take us to this newly created folder. It will then create the snap virtual environment and install Flask in this environment.

> Remember that the `mkvirtualenv` tool will create the virtual environment, which will be the default set of locations to install the packages from `pip`, but the `mkvirtualenv` command does not create the project folder for you. This is why we will run a command to create the project folder first and then create the virtual environment. Virtual environments, by virtue of the `$PATH` manipulation that is performed after the environments are activated, are completely independent of the location of your project files in the file system.

We will then create our basic blueprint-based project layout with an empty users blueprint. The contents of all the files are nearly the same as we described at the end of the previous chapter, and the layout should resemble the following:

```
application
├── __init__.py
├── run.py
└── users
    ├── __init__.py
    ├── models.py
    └── views.py
```

Flask-SQLAlchemy

Once the above files and folders have been created, we need to install the next important set of dependencies: SQLAlchemy, and the Flask extension that makes interacting with this library a bit more Flask-like, Flask-SQLAlchemy:

```
$ pip install flask-sqlalchemy
```

This will install the Flask extension to SQLAlchemy along with the base distribution of the latter and several other necessary dependencies in case they are not already present.

Now, if we were using a relational database system other than SQLite, this is the point where we would create the database entity in, say, PostgreSQL, along with the proper users and permissions so that our application can create tables and modify the contents of these tables. SQLite, however, does not require any of that. Instead, it assumes that any user that has access to the filesystem location of the database should also have permission to modify the contents of this database.

Later on in this chapter, we will see how the SQLite database file can be created automatically via SQLAlchemy. For the sake of completeness, however, here is how one would create an empty database in the current folder of your filesystem:

```
$ sqlite3 snap.db  # hit control-D to escape out of the interactive SQL
console if necessary.
```

As mentioned previously, we will be using SQLite as the database for our example applications and the directions given will assume that SQLite is being used; the exact name of the binary may differ on your system. You can substitute the equivalent commands to create and administer the database of your choice if anything other than SQLite is being used.

Now, we can begin the basic configuration of the Flask-SQLAlchemy extension.

Configuring Flask-SQLAlchemy

First, we must register the Flask-SQLAlchemy extension with the `application` object in the `application/__init__.py` file:

```python
from flask import Flask
from flask.ext.sqlalchemy import SQLAlchemy


app = Flask(__name__)


app.config['SQLALCHEMY_DATABASE_URI'] = 'sqlite:///../snap.db'
db = SQLAlchemy(app)
```

The value of `app.config['SQLALCHEMY_DATABASE_URI']` is the escaped relative path to the `snap.db` `SQLite` database that we created previously. Once this simple configuration is in place, we will be able to create the SQLite database automatically via the `db.create_all()` method, which can be invoked in an interactive Python shell:

```
$ python
>>>from application import db
>>>db.create_all()
```

This is an idempotent operation, which means that nothing would change even if the database already exists. If the local database file did not exist, however, it would be created. This also applies to adding new data models: running `db.create_all()` will add their definitions to the database, ensuring that the relevant tables have been created and are accessible. It does not, however, take into account the modification of an existing model/table definition that already exists in the database. For this, you will need to use the relevant tools (for example, the sqlite CLI, or a migration tool such as Alembic, which we discuss in a later chapter) to modify the corresponding table definitions to match those that have been updated in your models.

SQLAlchemy basics

SQLAlchemy is, first and foremost, a toolkit to interact with the relational databases in Python.

While it provides an incredible number of features — including the SQL connection handling and pooling for various database engines, ability to handle custom datatypes, and a comprehensive SQL expression API — the one feature that most developers are familiar with is the Object Relational Mapper. This mapper allows a developer to connect a Python object definition to a SQL table in the database of their choice, thus enabling them with the flexibility to control the domain models in their own application and requiring only minimal coupling to the database product and the engine-specific SQLisms that each of them exposes.

While debating the usefulness (or the lack thereof) of an object relational mapper is outside the scope of this chapter, for those who are unfamiliar with SQLAlchemy we will provide a list of benefits that using this tool brings to the table, as follows:

- Your domain models are written to interface with one of the most well-respected, tested, and deployed Python packages ever created — SQLAlchemy.

- Onboarding new developers to a project becomes an order of magnitude easier due to the extensive documentation, tutorials, books, and articles that have been written about using SQLAlchemy.

- The validation of queries is accomplished using the SQLAlchemy expression language at module import time instead of executing each query string against the database to determine if there is a syntax error present. The expression language is in Python and can thus be validated with your usual set of tools and IDE.

- Thanks to the implementation of design patterns such as the Unit of Work, the Identity Map, and various lazy loading features, the developer can often be saved from performing more database/network roundtrips than necessary. Considering that the majority of a request/response cycle in a typical web application can easily be attributed to network latency of one type or another, minimizing the number of database queries in a typical response is a net performance win on many fronts.

- While many successful, performant applications can be built entirely on the ORM, SQLAlchemy does not force it upon you. If, for some reason, it is preferable to write raw SQL query strings or to use the SQLAlchemy expression language directly, then you can do that and still benefit from the connection pooling and the Python DBAPI abstraction functionality that is the core of SQLAlchemy itself.

Now that we've given you several reasons why you should be using this database query and domain data abstraction layer, let's look at how we would go about defining a basic data model.

Declarative mapping and Flask-SQLAlchemy

SQLAlchemy implements a design pattern known as a **data mapper**. Fundamentally, the job of this data mapper is to bridge the definition and manipulation of a data model in code (in our case, Python class definitions) and the representation of this data model in a database. The mapper should know how code-related actions (for example, object construction, attribute modifications, and so on) relate to the SQL-specific statements in a database of our choice, ensuring that actions performed on our mapped Python objects are properly synchronized with the database table(s) they are linked to.

There are two ways in which we can integrate SQLAlchemy into our application: through the use of the declarative mapping that provides a consistent integration of tables, Python objects and the data mapper that glues them together, or by manually specifying these relations ourselves. Additionally, it is also possible to use the so-called SQLAlchemy "core", which eschews the data domain-centric approach for one based on the SQL expression language constructs that are included within SQLAlchemy.

For the purposes of this (and future) chapters, we will be utilizing the declarative approach.

To use the declarative mapping functionality, we need to ensure that any model classes that we define will inherit from the declarative base `Model` class that Flask-SQLAlchemy makes available to us (once we have initialized the extension):

```
from application import db


class User(db.Model):
    # model attributes
    pass
```

This `Model` class is, essentially, an instance of a `sqlalchemy.ext.declarative.declarative_base` class (with some additional defaults and useful functionalities), which provides the object with a metaclass that will handle the appropriate mapping constructs.

Once we have our model class definition in place, we will define the details about the related SQL table that will be mapped via the class-level attributes utilizing `Column` object instances. The first argument to a Column invocation is the type constraint that we want to impose on the attribute (which corresponds to a specific schema data type supported by the database), along with any optional arguments that the type supports, such as the size of the field. Additional arguments can be provided to indicate the constraints on the resulting table field definition:

```
class User(db.Model):

    id = db.Column(db.Integer, primary_key=True)
    email = db.Column(db.String(255), unique=True)
    username = db.Column(db.String(40), unique=True)
```

 As indicated previously, simply defining the attributes will not automatically translate into new tables and columns in our database. For this, we will need to call `db.create_all()` to initialize the table and column definitions.

We can easily create an instance of this model and assign some values to the attributes that we declared in our class definition:

```
$ (snap) python
>>>from application.users.models import User
>>>new_user = User(email="me@example.com", username="me")
```

```
>>>new_user.email
'me@example.com'
>>>new_user.username
'me'
```

 You may have noticed that our user model does not define a __init__ method, yet we are able to pass the email and username arguments to the object constructor when instantiating the above example. This is a feature of the SQLAlchemy declarative base class, which automatically assigns the named arguments at object construction time to their object attribute counterparts. As a result, defining a concrete constructor method for your data models is generally not necessary.

The instantiation of a model object does not imply that it has been persisted to the database. For that, we need to inform the SQLAlchemy session that we wish to add a new object to be tracked and have it committed to the database:

```
>>>from application import db
>>>db.session.add(new_user)
>>>db.session.commit()
```

Once the object has been committed, the id attribute will obtain the value of the primary key that the underlying database engine has assigned to it:

```
>>>print(new_user.id)
1
```

If we want to modify the value of an attribute, for example, change the e-mail address of a particular user, we simply need to assign the new value and then commit the change:

```
>>>new_user.email = 'new@example.com'
>>>db.session.add(new_user)
>>>db.session.commit()
>>>print(new_user.email)
u'new@example.com'
```

At this point, you may have noticed that there has not been a single line of SQL written for any of the previous operations and might be getting a bit concerned that the information embedded in the objects that you've created is not being persisted to the database. A cursory inspection of the database should put your mind at ease:

```
$ sqlite3 snap.db
SQLite version 3.8.5 2014-08-15 22:37:57
Enter ".help" for usage hints.
sqlite> .tables
user
sqlite> .schema user
CREATE TABLE user (
    id INTEGER NOT NULL,
    email VARCHAR(255),
    username VARCHAR(40),
    PRIMARY KEY (id),
    UNIQUE (email),
    UNIQUE (username)
);
sqlite> select * from user;
1|new@example.com|me
```

Remember that the exact name of the SQLite binary may differ on your operating system of choice. Additionally, if you chose a database engine other than SQLite to follow along with these examples, the relevant commands and results may be wildly different.

And there we have it: SQLAlchemy has successfully managed the relevant SQL INSERT and UPDATE statements behind the scenes, letting us work with native Python objects and signaling the session when we are ready to persist the data to the database.

We are not limited to defining class attributes, of course. In many instances it may prove useful to declare instance methods on our models so that we can perform more complex data manipulations. For example, imagine that we need to obtain the primary key ID of a given user and determine whether or not it is an even or odd integer. The method declaration would be just as you expect it to be:

```
class User(db.Model):

    id = db.Column(db.Integer, primary_key=True)
    email = db.Column(db.String(255), unique=True)
```

```
        username = db.Column(db.String(40), unique=True)

def is_odd_id(self):
        return (self.id % 2 != 0)
```

The instance method call can be performed as usual with the caveat that before the object is committed to the session, the primary key value will be none:

```
$ (snap)  python
Python 2.7.10 (default, Jul 13 2015, 23:27:37)
[GCC 4.2.1 Compatible Apple LLVM 6.1.0 (clang-602.0.53)] on darwin
Type "help", "copyright", "credits" or "license" for more information.
>>>fromapplication.users.models import User
>>>test = User(email='method@example.com', username='method_test')
>>>from application import db
>>>db.session.add(test)
>>>db.session.commit()
>>> test.id
2
>>>test.is_odd_id()
False
```

Of course, the preceding implementation is trivial and somewhat meaningless in the context of most web applications. However, the ability to define model instance methods in order to encode business logic is quite convenient and we will see some of this with the Flask-Login extension later on in this chapter.

Snap data models

Now that we've explored the basics of the SQLAlchemy declarative base and the Flask-SQLAlchemy extension using a somewhat simplified model, our next step is to flesh out a user data model that is the cornerstone of almost any web application. We'll create this model in the users blueprint in a new users/models.py module, and utilize the knowledge that we've gained regarding SQLAlchemy models to add the fields for a user password and a created_on field to store when the record was created. Additionally, we'll define a few instance methods:

```
import datetime
from application import db


class User(db.Model):
```

```python
    # The primary key for each user record.
    id = db.Column(db.Integer, primary_key=True)

    # The unique email for each user record.
    email = db.Column(db.String(255), unique=True)

    # The unique username for each record.
    username = db.Column(db.String(40), unique=True)

    # The hashed password for the user
    password = db.Column(db.String(60))

#   The date/time that the user account was created on.
    created_on = db.Column(db.DateTime,
        default=datetime.datetime.utcnow)


    def __repr__(self):
        return '<User {!r}>'.format(self.username)

    def is_authenticated(self):
        """All our registered users are authenticated."""
        return True

    def is_active(self):
        """All our users are active."""
        return True

    def is_anonymous(self):
        """We don)::f):lf):"""users are authenticated."""
        return False

    def get_id(self):
        """Get the user ID as a Unicode string."""
        return unicode(self.id)
```

The is_authenticated, is_active, is_anonymous, and get_id methods may seem arbitrary at the moment but are required for the next step, which will be installing and setting up the Flask-Login extension in order to help us manage our user authentication system.

Flask-Login and Flask-Bcrypt for authentication

As we've done several times already with other libraries, we will install the extensions in our current project's virtual environment:

```
$ (snap) pip install flask-login flask-bcrypt
```

The first is a Flask-specific library to normalize much of the standard user login process that nearly every web application requires, and the latter will allow us to ensure that the user passwords we store in our database are hashed using an industry standard algorithm.

Once installed, we need to instantiate and configure the extension in the usual manner. For this, we will add to the application/__init__.py module:

```
from flask import Flask
from flask.ext.sqlalchemy import SQLAlchemy
from flask.ext.login import LoginManager
from flask.ext.bcrypt import Bcrypt


app = Flask(__name__)


app.config['SQLALCHEMY_DATABASE_URI'] = 'sqlite:///../snap.db'
db = SQLAlchemy(app)


login_manager = LoginManager()
login_manager.init_app(app)
flask_bcrypt = Bcrypt(app)


from application.users import models as user_models
from application.users.views import users
```

In order to function correctly, the Flask-Login extension must also know how to load a user from your database given only the ID of this user. We must decorate a function that will accomplish this, and we'll insert it at the very end of the `application/__init__.py` module for the sake of simplicity:

```python
from flask import Flask
from flask.ext.sqlalchemy import SQLAlchemy
from flask.ext.login LoginManager
from flask.ext.bcrypt import Bcrypt


app = Flask(__name__)


app.config['SQLALCHEMY_DATABASE_URI'] = 'sqlite:///../snap.db'
db = SQLAlchemy(app)


login_manager = LoginManager()
login_manager.init_app(app)
flask_bcrypt = Bcrypt(app)


from application.users import models as user_models
from application.users.views import users



@login_manager.user_loader
def load_user(user_id):
    return application.user_models.query.get(int(user_id))
```

Now that we've set up the model and required methods/function so that Flask-Login can operate correctly, our next step will be to allow users to log in as they would on almost any web application using a form.

Flask-WTF – form validation and rendering

The Flask-WTF (`https://flask-wtf.readthedocs.org/en/latest/`) extension wraps the WTForms library , an incredibly flexible tool for managing and validating forms, and makes it readily available for use in Flask applications. Let's install this now and then we'll define our first form to handle user logins:

```
$ pip install flask-wtf
```

Next, we will define our first form in our `users/views.py` module:

```python
from flask import Blueprint

from flask.ext.wtf import Form
from wtforms import StringField, PasswordField
from wtforms.validators import DataRequired, Length


users = Blueprint('users', __name__, template_folder='templates')


classLoginForm(Form):
    """
    Represents the basic Login form elements & validators.
    """

    username = StringField('username', validators=[DataRequired()])
    password = PasswordField('password', validators=[DataRequired(),
        Length(min=6)])
```

Here we defined `LoginForm`, a subclass of `Form`, with the class attributes of `username` and `password`. The values of these attributes are `StringField` and `PasswordField`, each with their own set of validators to indicate that the form data of both fields is required to be non-empty and the password field itself should be at least six characters long in order to be considered valid.

Our `LoginForm` class will be utilized in two different ways, as follows:

- It will render the required form fields in our `login.html` template
- It will validate the POST'ed form data that we will require to complete a successful login from a user

To accomplish the first, we will need to define our HTML layout in `application/templates/layout.html`, using the Jinja2 templating language. Note the use of the `current_user` object proxy that is made available in all Jinja templates via the Flask-Login extension which allows us to determine whether the person who is browsing is already authenticated, and if so, then this person should be presented with a slightly different page content:

```html
<!doctype html>
<html>
  <head>
```

```
      <title>Snaps</title>
    </head>

    <body>
      <h1>Snaps</h1>

      {% for message in get_flashed_messages() %}
      <div class="flash">{{ message }}</div>
      {% endfor %}

      {% if not current_user.is_authenticated() %}
      <a href="{{ url_for('users.login') }}">login</a>
      {% else %}
      <a href="{{ url_for('users.logout') }}">logout</a>
      {% endif %}

      <div class="content">
      {% block content %}{% endblock %}
      </div>
    </body>
</html>
```

Now that we have our extremely basic layout, we need to create our `login.html` page at `application/users/templates/users/login.html`:

 The somewhat convoluted path of `application/users/templates/users/index.html` is required when using Blueprints due to the manner in which the default template loader searches the registered template paths; it allows for some relatively simple overriding of blueprint templates in your main application template folder at the cost of some additional file tree complexity.

```
{% extends "layout.html" %}

{% block content %}

<form action="{{ url_for('users.login')}}" method="post">
  {{ form.hidden_tag() }}
  {{ form.id }}
  <div>{{ form.username.label }}: {{ form.username }}</div>
  {% if form.username.errors %}
  <ul class="errors">{% for error in form.username.errors %}<li>{{
error }}</li>{% endfor %}</ul>
  {% endif %}
```

```
<div>{{ form.password.label }}: {{ form.password }}</div>
{% if form.password.errors %}
<ul class="errors">{% for error in form.password.errors %}<li>{{
error }}</li>{% endfor %}</ul>
{% endif %}

<div><input type="submit" value="Login"></div>
</form>


{% endblock %}
```

The preceding code will extend the basic application-level `layout.html` that we defined previously and insert the hidden form fields (required for the built-in CSRF protection that Flask-WTF offers), form labels, form inputs, and submit button. We will also display the inline errors returned to us by WTForms in the event that our submitted data does not pass our form validators for the fields in question.

> **Cross-Site Request Forgery (CSRF)** *is a type of attack that occurs when a malicious website, email, blog, instant message, or program causes a user's web browser to perform an unwanted action on a trusted site in which the user is currently authenticated. OWASP definition of CSRF*

The most common way of preventing a cross-site request forgery is to include a token with each HTML form that is sent to the user, which can then be validated against a matching token in the session of the authenticated user. If the token does not validate, then the form data is rejected, as there is a chance that the currently authenticated user did not willingly submit the form data in question.

Now that we have created the `login.html` template, we can next hook up a route view handler in `application/users/views.py` to process the login and form logic:

```
from flask import (Blueprint, flash, render_template, url_for, redirect,
g)
from flask.ext.login import login_user, logout_user, current_user

from flask.ext.wtf import Form
from wtforms import StringField, PasswordField
from wtforms.validators import DataRequired, Length

from models import User
```

```
from application import flask_bcrypt

users = Blueprint('users', __name__, template_folder='templates')


class LoginForm(Form):
    """
    Represents the basic Login form elements & validators.
    """

    username = StringField('username',
validators=[DataRequired()])
password = PasswordField('password',
validators=[DataRequired(),Length(min=6)])


@users.route('/login', methods=['GET', 'POST'])
def login():
    """
Basic user login functionality.

    If the user is already logged in , we
redirect the user to the default snaps index page.

    If the user is not already logged in and we have
form data that was submitted via POST request, we
call the validate_on_submit() method of the Flask-WTF
    Form object to ensure that the POST data matches what
we are expecting. If the data validates, we login the
user given the form data that was provided and then
redirect them to the default snaps index page.

    Note: Some of this may be simplified by moving the actual User
loading and password checking into a custom Flask-WTF validator
for the LoginForm, but we avoid that for the moment, here.
    """

current_user.is_authenticated():
```

```
        return redirect(url_for('snaps.listing))


    form = LoginForm()
    if form.validate_on_submit():

        user = User.query.filter_by(
            username=form.username.data).first()

        if not user:
            flash("No such user exists.")
            returnrender_template('users/login.html', form=form)

        if(not flask_bcrypt.check_password_hash(user.password,
            form.password.data)):

            flash("Invalid password.")
            returnrender_template('users/login.html', form=form)

        login_user(user, remember=True)
        flash("Success!  You're logged in.")
        returnredirect(url_for("snaps.listing"))

    return render_template('users/login.html', form=form)



@users.route('/logout', methods=['GET'])
def logout():
    logout_user()
    return redirect(url_for(('snaps.listing')))
```

Hashing user passwords

We will update our user model in order to ensure that the passwords are encrypted
by Flask-Bcrypt when the password field is updated. In order to accomplish this,
we will use a feature of SQLAlchemy that is similar in spirit and functionality to the
Python @property decorator (and the associated property.setter method), named
hybrid attributes.

Hybrid attributes are so named because they can provide distinctly different behaviors when invoked at the class level or instance level. The SQLAlchemy documentation is a great place to learn about the various roles that they can fulfill in your domain modeling.

We will simply rename the password class-level attribute with _password so that our hybrid attribute methods do not conflict. Subsequently, we add the hybrid attribute methods which encapsulate the password hashing logic on attribute assignment:

 In addition to the hybrid property approach, our requirements for password hashing on assignment could also be satisfied using a SQLAlchemy TypeDecorator, which allows us to augment the existing types (for example, a String column type) with additional behaviors.

```python
import datetime
from application import db, flask_bcrypt
from sqlalchemy.ext.hybrid import hybrid_property




class User(db.Model):

    # ...

    # The hashed password for the user
    _password = db.Column('password', db.String(60))

    # ...
    @hybrid_property
    def password(self):
        """The bcrypt'ed password of the given user."""

return self._password

  @password.setter
  def password(self, password):
      """Bcrypt the password on assignment."""
```

```
        self._password = flask_bcrypt.generate_password_hash(
            password)

    # ...
```

In order to generate a user for testing purposes (and to verify that our password was hashed on instance construction/attribute assignment), let's load the Python console and create a user instance ourselves using the model that we defined and the SQLAlchemy database connection that we created:

 Remember to initialize the database with `db.create_all()` if you `haven't already`.

```
>>>from application.users.models import User
>>>user = User(username='test', password='mypassword', email='test@
example.com')
>>>user.password
'$2a$12$06oHgytOVz1hrUyoknlgqeG7TiVS7M.ogRPv4YJgAJyVeUIV8ad2i'
>>>from application import db
>>>db.session.add(user)
>>>db.session.commit()
```

Configure an application SECRET_KEY

The last little bit that we need is to define an application-wide SECRET_KEY that will be used by Flask-WTF to sign a token to be used for the prevention of CSRF attacks. We will add this key to the application configuration in application/__init__.py:

```
from flask import Flask
fromflask.ext.sqlalchemy import SQLAlchemy
fromflask.ext.login import LoginManager
fromflask.ext.bcrypt import Bcrypt


app = Flask(__name__)


app.config['SQLALCHEMY_DATABASE_URI'] = 'sqlite:///../snap.db'
app.config['SECRET_KEY'] = "-80:,bPrVzTXp*zXZ0[9T/ZT=1ej08"
# ...
```

Of course, you'll want to use your own unique secret key; the easiest way to accomplish this would be to use your system kernel's random number device via /dev/urandom, available for most Linux distributions. In python, you can use the os.urandom method to get a random string with *n* bytes of entropy.

Hook up the blueprint

Before we can run the application, we need to register our newly created users blueprint with the Flask application object. This necessitates a slight modification to application/__init__.py:

```
from flask import Flask
from flask.ext.sqlalchemy import SQLAlchemy
from flask.ext.login import LoginManager
from flask.ext.bcrypt import Bcrypt


app = Flask(__name__)


# ...
from application.users.views import users
app.register_blueprint(users, url_prefix='/users')


# ...
```

Let's run this thing

Now that we've put all the little pieces together, let's run the application and make things happen. We will use a similar run.py file that we used in the previous chapter, which has been adapted to work with our application factory:

```
from application import create_app


app = create_app(config='settings')
app.run(debug=True)
```

This file is placed as a sibling to the application folder and then invoked in the usual way:

```
$ python run.py
```

Visit `http://localhost:5000/users/login` and you should be presented with the `username` and `password` input fields that we created. If you attempt to input invalid fields (for example, a username that does not exist), the page will render with the relevant error message. If you attempt to log in with the user credentials that we created at the interactive prompt earlier, then you should be greeted with the text: `Success! You logged in.`

The data model for snaps

Now that we've created our bare bones user models, view functions, and hooked up our authentication system, let's create the model required to store our Snaps in a new blueprint, under `application/snaps/models.py`.

 Don't forget to create `application/snaps/__init__.py`, otherwise the folder will not be recognized as a package!

This model will be very similar to our User model but will contain additional information regarding the relationships between a user and their snaps. In SQLAlchemy, we will describe the relations between records in tables via the use of `ForeignKey` objects and the `relationship` methods:

```
import datetime
import hashlib
from application import db


class Snap(db.Model):

    # The primary key for each snap record.
    id = db.Column(db.Integer, primary_key=True)

    # The name of the file; does not need to be unique.
    name = db.Column(db.String(128))

    # The extension of the file; used for proper syntax
    # highlighting
    extension = db.Column(db.String(12))

    # The actual content of the snap
```

```
    content = db.Column(db.Text())

    # The unique, un-guessable ID of the file
    hash_key = db.Column(db.String(40), unique=True)

    #  The date/time that the snap was created on.
    created_on = db.Column(db.DateTime,
        default=datetime.datetime.utcnow,index=True)

    # The user this snap belongs to
    user_id = db.Column(db.Integer, db.ForeignKey('user.id'))

    user = db.relationship('User', backref=db.backref(
        'snaps', lazy='dynamic'))

    def __init__(self, user_id, name, content, extension):
        """
        Initialize the snap object with the required attributes.
        """

        self.user_id = user_id
        self.name = name
        self.content = content
        self.extension = extension

self.created_on = datetime.datetime.utcnow()

        # This could be made more secure by combining the
        # application SECRET_KEYin the hash as a salt.
            self.hash_key = hashlib.sha1(self.content + str(self.created_
on)).hexdigest()


    def __repr__(self):
        return '<Snap {!r}>'.format(self.id)
```

Most of this model should be relatively familiar; it is not that much different from the one we constructed previously for our User schema. For our snaps, we will require a few mandatory attributes, as follows:

- `user_id`: This is the ID of the user who has created the snap. As our current implementation will require a user to be authenticated in order to create a snap, all the resulting snaps will be tied to the user who posted them. This will also make it trivial to extend the system at a later time so as to include the user profiles, personal snap statistics, and ability to delete a snap.
- `created_on`: This is set in the constructor to be the current UTC timestamp and will be used to sort the snaps in descending order to display them in a list on our landing page.
- `hash_key`: This attribute is also set in the constructor and is the cryptographic hash of the contents of the snap concatenated with the timestamp it was created on. This gives us a unique, secure ID that is not easily guessable that we can use in order to refer to the snap at a later time.

 Even though the conditions that we described for the preceding `hash_key` do not guarantee that the value is unique, The uniqueness of the snap hash key is also enforced at the database level via a unique index constraint.

- `content`: This is the content of the snap itself — the meat and potatoes of the model.
- `extension`: This is the file extension of the snap, so that we can include simple syntax highlighting if we so desire.
- `name`: This is the name of the snap, which is not required to be unique.
- `user`: This is a special attribute to declare that every snap instance is related to a user instance and will allow us to access the data of the user who has created a snap. The `backref` option also specifies that the reverse should be possible: that is, accessing all the snaps created by a user via the snaps attribute on a user instance.

Better defaults with content-sensitive default functions

One improvement that can be made to the preceding model is the removal of the explicit __init__ method. The only reason that it was defined initially was to ensure that the hash_key field could be constructed from the value of the content field. While in most instances the explicit object constructor that was defined would be good enough, SQLAlchemy provides us with the functionality that will allow us to set the default value of one field based on the contents of another. This is known as a **Context–Sensitive Default Function** and can be declared as such at the top of the application/snaps/models.py module:

```python
defcontent_hash(context):
    # This could be made more secure by combining the
    # application SECRET_KEY in the hash as a salt.
    content = context.current_parameters['content']
    created_on = context.current_parameters['created_on']
    return hashlib.sha1(content + str(created_on)).hexdigest()
```

Once this method exists, we can define the default argument of the hash_key column to be our content_hash content-sensitive default:

```python
# The unique, un-guessable ID of the file
hash_key = db.Column(db.String(40), unique=True,
    default=content_hash)
```

Snap view handlers

Continuing on, we will now create the views and templates that are required to list and add snaps. To this end, we will instantiate a Blueprint object in our application/snaps/views.py and declare our route handlers:

```python
from flask import Blueprint
from flask.ext.login import login_required


from .models import Snap


snaps = Blueprint('snaps', __name__, template_folder='templates')


@snaps.route('/', methods=['GET'])
```

```
def listing():
"""List all snaps; most recent first."""


@snaps.route('/add', methods=['GET', 'POST'])
@login_required
def add():
    """Add a new snap."""
```

Note that we have wrapped our add() route handler with a @login_required decorator, which will prevent unauthenticated users from accessing this endpoint for all defined HTTP verbs (GET and POST, in this case) and return a 401.

 Instead of having the server return an HTTP 401 Unauthorized, Flask-Login can be configured to redirect the unauthenticated user to the login page by setting the login_manager.login_ view attribute to the url_for compatible location of the login page itself, which in our case would be users.login.

Now, let's create the WTForm object to represent a snap and place it in the application/snaps/views.py module:

```
from flask.ext.wtf import Form
from wtforms import StringField
from wtforms.widgets import TextArea
from wtforms.validators import DataRequired


class SnapForm(Form):
    """Form for creating new snaps."""

    name = StringField('name', validators=[DataRequired()])
    extension = StringField('extension',
        validators=[DataRequired()])
    content = StringField('content', widget=TextArea(),
        validators=[DataRequired()])
```

While it is somewhat a matter of personal preference, the forms created with WTForms (or any other similar abstraction) could be placed alongside the models instead of the views. Or, to go a step further, if you have many different forms with complex data relationships, it may also be advisable to put all the declared forms in their own module in your application.

Our snaps require a name, an extension, and the content of the snap itself, and we've encapsulated these basic requirements in the preceding Form declaration. Let's implement our `add()` route handler:

```python
from flask import Blueprint, render_template, url_for, redirect, current_
app, flash
from flask.ext.login import login_required, current_user
from sqlalchemy import exc


from .models import Snap
from application import db


# ...


@snaps.route('/add', methods=['GET', 'POST'])
@login_required
def add():
    """Add a new snap."""

    form = SnapForm()

    if form.validate_on_submit():
        user_id = current_user.id

        snap = Snap(user_id=user_id, name=form.name.data,
            content=form.content.data,
            extension=form.extension.data)
        db.session.add(snap)

try:
```

```
db.session.commit()

    except exc.SQLAlchemyError:

        current_app.exception("Could not save new snap!")

        flash("Something went wrong while posting your snap!")


    else:

        return render_template('snaps/add.html', form=form)


    return redirect(url_for('snaps.listing'))
```

Briefly, we will validate the submitted POST data in order to ensure that it satisfies the validators that we specified in the `SnapForm` class declaration and then proceed to instantiate a `Snap` object with the supplied form data and ID of the currently authenticated user. Once built, we will add this object to the current SQLAlchemy session and then attempt to commit it to the database. If a SQLAlchemy exception occurs (all SQLAlchemy exceptions inherit from `salalchemy.exc.SQLALchemyError`), we will log an exception to the default application log handler and set a flash message so that the user is alerted that something unexpected has occurred.

For the sake of completeness, we will include the extremely simple `application/snaps/templates/snaps/add.html` Jinja template here:

```
{% extends "layout.html" %}


{% block content %}
<form action="{{ url_for('snaps.add') }}" method="post">

    {{ form.hidden_tag() }}
    {{ form.id }}

    <div class="row">
        <div>{{ form.name.label() }}: {{ form.name }}</div>
        {% if form.name.errors %}
        <ul class="errors">{% for error in form.name.errors %}<li>{{ error
}}</li>{% endfor %}</ul>
        {% endif %}

        <div>{{ form.extension.label() }}: {{ form.extension }}</div>
        {% if form.extension.errors %}
        <ul class="errors">{% for error in form.extension.errors %}<li>{{
error }}</li>{% endfor %}</ul>
        {% endif %}
```

```
    </div>

    <div class="row">
      <div>{{ form.content.label() }}: {{ form.content }}</div>
      {% if form.content.errors %}
      <ul class="errors">{% for error in form.content.errors %}<li>{{
error }}</li>{% endfor %}</ul>
      {% endif %}
    </div>

    <div><input type="submit" value="Snap"></div>
  </form>

  {% endblock %}
```

Once we've completed the `add()` handler and associated template, now it's time to move on to the `listing()` handler, which will incidentally be the landing page for our application. The listing page will, somewhat unimaginatively, show a listing of the 20 most recent snaps which have been posted, in reverse chronological order:

```
@snaps.route('/', methods=['GET'])

def listing():
    """List all snaps; most recent first."""
    snaps = Snap.query.order_by(
        Snap.created_on.desc()).limit(20).all()
    return render_template('snaps/index.html', snaps=snaps)
```

The `application/snaps/templates/snaps/add.html` Jinja template renders the snaps that we've queried from the database:

```
  {% extends "layout.html" %}


  {% block content %}
  <div class="new-snap">
    <p><a href="{{url_for('snaps.add')}}">New Snap</a></p>
  </div>

  {% for snap in snaps %}
  <div class="snap">
    <span class="author">{{snap.user.username}}</span>, published on
  <span class="date">{{snap.created_on}}</span>
    <pre><code>{{snap.content}}</code></pre>
  </div>
```

```
{% endfor %}

{% endblock %}
```

Next, we must ensure that the snaps blueprint that we've created is loaded in the application and prefixed to the root/URI path by adding it to the `application/__init__.py` module:

```
from flask import Flask
from flask.ext.sqlalchemy import SQLAlchemy
from flask.ext.login import LoginManager
from flask.ext.bcrypt import Bcrypt


# ...


from application.users import models as user_models
from application.users.views import users
from application.snaps.views import snaps


app.register_blueprint(users, url_prefix='/users')
app.register_blueprint(snaps, url_prefix='')



@login_manager.user_loader
de fload_user(user_id):
    return user_models.User.query.get(int(user_id))
```

In order to test our new functionality, we'll need to add the newly created snap model to our database. We can accomplish this by executing the `db.create_all()` function that we described earlier in the chapter. As we tend to run this command quite a lot, let's put it in a script sibling to our main application package folder and name the file `database.py`:

```
from application import db
db.create_all()
```

Once in place, we can simply execute the script with the Python interpreter in order to create the new snap model in our database:

```
$ python database.py
```

Now that our database should be up to date with our model definitions, let's ensure that the application runs as expected:

```
$ python run.py
```

Assuming that there were no errors, you should be able to visit the URL that is displayed and log in with the credentials of one of the users that we created earlier in the chapter. You can, of course, create a new user via the interactive Python interpreter and then use these credentials so as to test the authentication functionality of the application:

```
$ python
>>>from application import db
>>>from application.users.models import User
>>>user = User(name='test', email='test@example.com', password='foobar')
>>>db.session.add(user)
>>>db.session.commit(user)
```

Summary

After having gone through this chapter and building the Snap application, we have seen several facets of how Flask may be augmented with the use of extensions, such as Flask-WTF (for web form creation and validation), Flask-SQLAlchemy (for simple integration with the SQLAlchemy database abstraction library), Flask-Bcrypt (for password hashing), and Flask-Login (to abstract much of the standard implementation requirements for a simple user login system). While Flask itself is relatively spartan, the ecology of extensions that are available make it such that building a fully fledged user-authenticated application may be done quickly and relatively painlessly.

We explored the aforementioned extensions and their usefulness, including Flask-WTF and Flask-SQLAlchemy, and architected a simple blueprint-based application that integrated all of the above components. While the Snap application itself is quite simple and leaves much to be implemented, it lends itself very easily to updates and additional features.

In the next chapter, we will build an application with a more complex data model and include some social features that are common among today's web apps. Moreover, it will be built and set up for unit and functional testing, something that no trivial application should go without.

4
Socializer – the Testable Timeline

In this chapter we will build our next application with the codename: Socializer. This application will provide you with a very typical *timeline* feed, whose variations grace many well-known modern web applications.

This application will allow authenticated users to follow others, and be followed by other users, and display content posted from the followed users in a time-ordered fashion. Along with building the basic features required of a timeline-based application, we will implement additional behaviors using the excellent `Blinker` library for in-process publish/subscribe signals that will allow us to decouple the application into more compassable, reusable parts.

Additionally, Socializer will be built with unit and functional testing in mind, allowing us to vigorously test the various models and views to ensure that it functions according to our expectations.

Starting off

As we did in the previous chapter, let's create a completely new directory for this application, in addition to creating a virtual environment and installing a few basic packages that we will be using:

```
$ mkdir -p ~/src/socializer && cd ~/src/socializer
$ mkvirtualenv socializer
$ pip install flask flask-sqlalchemy flask-bcrypt flask-login flask-wtf
blinker pytest-flask
```

Our application layout will, for the moment, be very similar to the one that we used in the previous chapter:

```
├── application
│   ├── __init__.py
│   └── users
│       ├── __init__.py
│       ├── models.py
│       └── views.py
└── run.py
└── database.py
```

Application factories

One of the major benefits of unit and functional testing is the ability to ensure, under a variety of different conditions and configurations, that your application behaves in a known and predictable manner. To this end, it will be a great advantage to have the ability to construct all the Flask application objects in our test suite. We can then easily provide different configurations to each of these objects and ensure that they exhibit the behavior that we expect.

Thankfully, this is entirely achievable using the application factory pattern, which is well supported by Flask. Let's add a `create_app` method to our `application/__init__.py` module:

```python
from flask import Flask


def create_app(config=None):
    app = Flask(__name__)

    if config is not None:
        app.config.from_object(config)


    return app
```

What this method does is relatively simple: given an optional `config` argument, construct a Flask application object, optionally apply this custom configuration, and finally return the newly created Flask application object to the caller.

Previously, we would simply instantiate a Flask object in the module itself, which meant that on import of this package or module the application object would be immediately available. However, this also meant that there was no simple way of doing the following:

- Delaying the construction of the application object to some time after the module was imported to the local namespace. This may seem frivolous at first but is incredibly useful and powerful for large applications that can benefit from this type of lazy instantiation. As we mentioned previously, side-effect generating package imports should be avoided as much as possible.

- Substituting different application configuration values, such as those that may be needed while running tests. We might like to avoid, for example, sending out e-mail notifications to real world users while running our test suite.

- Running multiple Flask applications in the same process. While we do not explicitly address the concept in this book, this can be useful in a variety of situations, such as having separate application instances that serve different versions of a public API or separate application objects that serve different content types (JSON, XML, and so on). More information on this topic can be gleaned from the *Application dispatching* section in the official Flask online documentation http://flask.pocoo.org/docs/0.10/patterns/appdispatch/.

With the application factory, we now have more flexibility in when and how our main application object is constructed. The downside (or upside, if you're intent on running several applications in the same process!), of course, is that we no longer have access to a quasi-global `app` object that we can import to our modules in order to do things such as register route handlers or access the `app` object's logger.

The application context

One of the principal design goals of Flask is to ensure that you can run multiple applications in the same Python process. How, then, should an application be certain that the `app` object being imported to a module is the correct one and not the object for one of the other applications running in the same process?

In other frameworks that support the single-process/multi-app paradigm, this is sometimes accomplished by enforcing explicit dependency injection: a code that requires an `app` object to be present should explicitly require that the app object be passed to the function or method that needs it. From an architectural design perspective this sounds great, but this can quickly become cumbersome if third-party libraries or extensions do not follow the same design principles. At best, you will end up needing to write a lot of boilerplate wrapper functions, and at worst you will end up resorting to monkey-patching modules and classes in a never-ending downward spiral of brittleness and unnecessary complexity that will ultimately cause you more trouble than you originally bargained for.

> There is, of course, nothing inherently wrong with explicit dependency injection boilerplate wrapper functions. Flask has simply chosen a different approach, which it has been criticized for in the past, but has shown to be both flexible, testable, and resilient.

Flask, for better or worse, has been built around an alternative method that is based on proxy objects. These proxy objects are, in essence, container objects that are shared among all the threads and know how to dispatch to the *real* objects that are bound to a particular thread behind the scenes.

> A common misconception is that in a threaded application, each request will be assigned its own new thread under the WSGI specification: this is simply not the case. New requests may reuse existing but currently unused threads, and this old thread may have locally scoped variables still lurking around that may interfere with your new request handling.

One of these proxy objects, `current_app`, is created and bound to the current request This means that instead of importing an already-constructed Flask application object (or worse, creating additional application objects in the same request), we replace it with the following:

```
from flask import current_app as app
```

> The aliasing of the imported `current_app` object is, of course, completely optional. It is sometimes preferable to leave it named `current_app` so as to remind yourself that it is not the real application object, but a proxy to it.

Using this proxy object, we can sidestep the issue of not having an instantiated Flask application object available to us at import time when we implement the application factory pattern.

Instantiating an app object

Of course, at some point, we need to actually create an application object so that the proxies have something to, well, proxy to. Generally, we want to create the object once and then we want to make sure that the run method is invoked in order to launch the Werkzeug development server.

To this end, we can modify the run.py script that we had in the previous chapter to instantiate the app object from our factory and invoke the run method on the newly created instance, as follows:

```
from application import create_app


app = create_app()
app.run(debug=True)
```

Now, we should be able to run this extremely barebones application as we have previously done:

```
$ python run.py
```

 It is also possible to invoke the Python interpreter such that a module, package, or script is imported to the environment for you and executed immediately. This is accomplished with the -m flag and our preceding invocation of run.py can be modified to the more concise version, as follows:

```
$ python -m run
```

Unit and functional testing

One of the primary benefits of implementing an application factory to hand out the Flask application instances is that we have the abilities to test the application more effectively. We can construct different application instances for different test cases and can be sure that they are as isolated from each other as possible (or as much as Flask/Werkzeug will allow).

The mainstay of the testing libraries in the Python ecosystem is unittest, which is included in the standard library and includes much of the functionalities that are expected of an xUnit framework. While a complete exposition on unittest is largely out of the scope of this book, a typical class-based test case will follow this basic skeleton, assuming that we are still using the factory pattern to separate our application configuration from instantiation:

```python
from myapp import create_app
import unittest


class AppTestCase(unittest.TestCase):

    def setUp(self):
        app = create_app()   # Could also pass custom settings.
        app.config['TESTING'] = True
        self.app = app

        # Whatever DB initialization is required

    def tearDown(self):
        # If anything needs to be cleaned up after a test.
        Pass

    def test_app_configuration(self):
        self.assertTrue(self.app.config['TESTING'])
        # Other relevant assertions


if __name__ == '__main__':
    unittest.main()
```

The following are the advantages of using the unittest test format/style:

- It does not require external dependencies; unittest is part of the Python standard library.
- Getting started is relatively easy. Most xUnit testing frameworks follow similar naming conventions to declare the test classes and test methods, and include several helpers for typical assertions such as assertTrue or assertEqual, among several others.

It is, however, not the only player in town; we will be using `pytest` and the associated Flask extension that wraps the convenient functionality, `pytest-flask`.

In addition to being a slightly more modern and concise testing framework, the other major advantage that `pytest` provides over many other testing tools is the ability to define fixtures for the tests, which are described quite succinctly from their own documentation, as follows:

- Fixtures have explicit names and are activated by declaring their use from test functions, modules, classes, or whole projects

- Fixtures are implemented in a modular manner as each fixture name triggers a fixture function that itself can use other fixtures

- Fixture management scales from a simple unit to complex functional testing, allowing you to parameterize fixtures and tests according to the configuration and component options or to reuse fixtures across class, module, or whole test session scopes

In the context of testing a Flask application, this means that we can define objects (such as our application object) in a `fixture` and then have this object automatically injected into a test function via the use of an argument that has the same name as the defined fixture function.

If that last paragraph was a bit too much to handle, then a simple example should be enough to clear things up. Let's create the following `conftest.py` file, which will contain any test suite-wide fixtures and helpers that our other tests might use:

```
import pytest
from application import create_app



@pytest.fixture
def app():
    app = create_app()
    return app
```

We will create our first test module in `tests/test_application.py`, as follows:

 Note that the `tests_*` prefix to the test file names is important—it allows `pytest` to automatically discover which files contain test functions and assertions that need to be run. If a filename in your tests/folder does not have the aforementioned prefix, then the test runner will abstain from loading it and treating it as a file that contains functions with test assertions.

```
import flask


def test_app(app):

    assert isinstance(app, flask.Flask)
```

 Note that the app argument in the test_app function signature matches the name of the app fixture function that is defined in conftest.py, and the value that is passed to test_app is the return value of the app fixture function.

We will run the test suite using the py.test executable that was installed to our virtual environment (when we added the pytest-flask and pytest libraries) in the directory that contains conftest.py and our tests/folder, and the output will indicate that our test module was discovered and run:

```
$ py.test
=============== test session starts ================
platform darwin -- Python 2.7.8 -- py-1.4.26 -- pytest-2.7.0
rootdir: /path/to/socializer, inifile:
plugins: flask
collected 1 items

tests/test_application.py .

============== 1 passed in 0.02 seconds ==============
```

And that's it! We've written and run our very first, albeit uninteresting, test for our application. Don't fret if you don't quite understand what's going on just yet; quite a bit of concrete testing is coming up in this chapter and many more examples will follow.

Social features – friends and followers

Many modern web applications allow users to *friend* or *follow* other users and be friended or followed themselves. While this concept may be simple to explain in words, there are numerous implementations and variations, all of which are optimized for their particular use-cases.

In this situation, where we want to implement a newsfeed-like service that displays information from a selected pool of users in an aggregated timeline that is unique for each authenticated user, the following are the three categories of approaches that may be used:

- **Fan-out on Write**: Each newsfeed for a user is stored in a separate logical container with the intention of making reads exceedingly simple, fast, and straightforward, at the expense of denormalization and lower write throughput. The logical container may be a database table for each user (although this is highly inefficient for a large amount of users), columns in a column-oriented database such as Cassandra, or more specialized storage solutions such as Redis lists that may have elements added to them in an atomic fashion.

- **Fan-out on Read**: When newsfeeds require additional customization or processing to determine things such as visibility or relevance, a fan-out on read approach is usually best. This allows more fine-grained control over which items will end up in the feed and in which order (assuming that something more elaborate than chronological is required) at the cost of increased computational time to load the user-specific feed. Such a costly approach may be mitigated by keeping the recent items in RAM (which is the basic approach behind the Facebook™ newsfeed and the reason why Facebook also has the largest deployment of Memcache in the world), but this introduces several layers of complexity and indirection.

- **Naïve Normalization**: This is the least scalable of the approaches, but the simplest to implement. For many small-scale applications, this is the best place to start: a post's table that contains all the items created by users (with a foreign key constraint to the user who created that particular item) and a follower's table that tracks which users are following whom. Various caching solutions may be used to speed up parts of the request at the cost of additional complexity and may be introduced when they are necessary.

For the purposes of our Socializer application, the third approach, the so-called naïve normalization, will be the one we implement. The other approaches are valid, and you may choose to go down either path depending on your goals, but for the sake of simplicity and exposition we shall choose the one that requires the least amount of work.

With this in mind, let's begin by implementing the basic SQLAlchemy models and relationships that are required. First, let's use our newly minted application factory to initialize and configure the Flask-SQLAlchemy extension along with Flask-Bcrypt to hash our user passwords, using the same hybrid property approach that we explored in the previous chapter. Our `application/__init__.py` is as follows:

```
from flask import Flask
from flask.ext.sqlalchemy import SQLAlchemy
from flask.ext.bcrypt import Bcrypt


# Initialize the db extension, but without configuring
```

```
# it with an application instance.
db = SQLAlchemy()


# The same for the Bcrypt extension
flask_bcrypt = Bcrypt()



def create_app(config=None):
    app = Flask(__name__)

    if config is not None:
        app.config.from_object(config)

    # Initialize any extensions and bind blueprints to the
    # application instance here.
    db.init_app(app)
    flask_bcrypt.init_app(app)


    return app
```

Due to the use of the application factory, we separated the instantiation of the extensions (db and flask_bcrypt) from their configurations. The former happens at the time of import and the latter needs to occur when the Flask application object is constructed. Luckily, most modern Flask extensions allow this exact separation to occur, as we have demonstrated in the preceding snippet.

Now, we will create our user's package by creating application/users/__init__.py, then we will create application/users/models.py with our standard bits for the Flask-Login extension (which we will use later) as we did in the previous chapter. In addition, we will add an explicit SQLAlchemy mapping for our follower's table and the following associated relationship on the User model:

```
import datetime
from application import db, flask_bcrypt
from sqlalchemy.ext.hybrid import import hybrid_property


__all__ = ['followers', 'User']


# We use the explicit SQLAlchemy mappers for declaring the
# followers table, since it does not require any of the features
```

```
# that the declarative base model brings to the table.
#
# The `follower_id` is the entry that represents a user who
# *follows* a `user_id`.
followers = db.Table(
    'followers',
    db.Column('follower_id', db.Integer, db.ForeignKey('user.id'),
        primary_key=True),
    db.Column('user_id', db.Integer, db.ForeignKey('user.id'),
        primary_key=True))


class User(db.Model):

    # The primary key for each user record.
    id = db.Column(db.Integer, primary_key=True)

    # The unique email for each user record.
    email = db.Column(db.String(255), unique=True)

    # The unique username for each record.
    username = db.Column(db.String(40), unique=True)

    # The hashed password for the user
    _password = db.Column('password', db.String(60))
    #   The date/time that the user account was created on.
    created_on = db.Column(db.DateTime,
        default=datetime.datetime.utcnow)

    followed = db.relationship('User',
        secondary=followers,
        primaryjoin=(id==followers.c.follower_id ),
        secondaryjoin=(id==followers.c.user_id),
        backref=db.backref('followers', lazy='dynamic'),
        lazy='dynamic')

    @hybrid_property
    def password(self):
        """The bcrypt'ed password of the given user."""
```

```
        return self._password

    @password.setter
    def password(self, password):
        """Bcrypt the password on assignment."""

        self._password = flask_bcrypt.generate_password_hash(
            password)

    def __repr__(self):
        return '<User %r>' % self.username

    def is_authenticated(self):
        """All our registered users are authenticated."""
        return True

    def is_active(self):
        """All our users are active."""
        return True

    def is_anonymous(self):
        """We don't have anonymous users; always False"""
        return False
    def get_id(self):
        """Get the user ID."""
        return unicode(self.id)
```

The `followed` attribute of the User model is a SQLAlchemy relationship that maps the user's table to itself via the intermediate follower's table. The intermediate table is necessary due to the implicit many-to-many relationship that a social connection requires. Take a close look at the `followed` attribute, as shown in the following code:

```
followed = db.relationship('User',
    secondary=followers,
    primaryjoin=(id==followers.c.follower_id ),
    secondaryjoin=(id==followers.c.user_id),
    backref=db.backref('followers', lazy='dynamic'),
    lazy='dynamic')
```

We can see that the declaration is somewhat complex in comparison to the regular column definitions that we used in this chapter and in previous ones. However, each argument to the `relationship` function has a very definite purpose, as shown in the following list:

- `User`: This is the string-based name of the target relationship class. This can also be the mapped class itself, but then you might end up in a quagmire of circular import problems.

- `primaryjoin`: The value of this argument will be evaluated and then used as the `join` condition for the primary table (`user`) to the association table (`follower`).

- `secondaryjoin`: The value of this argument, similar to the `primaryjoin`, is evaluated and then used in the `join` condition of the association table (`follower`) to the child table (`user`). As our primary and child tables are one and the same (users follow other users), this condition is almost identical to the one produced in the `primaryjoin` argument, differing only in the key that is mapped in the association table.

- `backref`: This is the name of the property that will be inserted on an instance that will handle the reverse direction of the relationship. This means that once we have a user instance, we can access `user.followers` to get the list of people that are following the given user instance, as opposed to the `user.followed` attribute in which we explicitly define the list of users that the current user is following.

- `lazy`: This is the most often misused attribute for any relationship-based property. There are various values available, ranging from `select`, `immediate`, `joined`, `subquery`, `noload`, and `dynamic`. These determine how or when the related data is loaded. For our application, we've chosen to use the value of dynamic, which, instead of returning an iterable collection, returns a `Query` object that can then be further refined and acted on. For example, we can do something such as `user.followed.filter(User.username == 'example')`. While this is not very useful in this particular instance, it provides a huge amount of flexibility, sometimes at the cost of generating less efficient SQL queries.

The various attributes that we will set are to ensure that the generated queries use the correct columns to create the self-referential many-to-many join and the query to obtain the list of followers is only executed when we need it. More information about these particular patterns can be found in the official SQLAlchemy documentation: `http://docs.sqlalchemy.org/en/latest/`.

Now, we will add a few methods to our User model that will facilitate the following/unfollowing of other users. Thanks to some under-the-hood cleverness from SQLAlchemy, adding and removing followers for a user can be expressed as if you were acting on a native Python list, as follows:

```python
def unfollow(self, user):
    """
    Unfollow the given user.

    Return `False` if the user was not already following the user.
    Otherwise, remove the user from the followed list and return
    the current object so that it may then be committed to the
    session.
    """

    if not self.is_following(user):
        return False

    self.followed.remove(user)
    return self


def follow(self, user):
    """
    Follow the given user.
    Return `False` if the user was already following the user.
    """

    if self.is_following(user):
        return False

    self.followed.append(user)
    return self


def is_following(self, user):
    """
    Returns boolean `True` if the current user is following the
    given `user`, and `False` otherwise.
    """
    followed = self.followed.filter(followers.c.user_id == user.id)
    return followed.count() > 0
```

In reality, you are not acting on a native Python list, but rather a data structure that SQLAlchemy knows how to track the removals and additions from and then synchronize these to the database via the Unit of Work pattern.

Next, we will create the `Post` model and we'll do so in the blueprint module of `application/posts/models.py`. As usual, don't forget to create the `application/posts/__init__.py` file in order to declare the folder as a valid Python package, otherwise some very confusing import errors will occur when you attempt to run the application.

For now, this particular model will be a paragon of simplicity. Here's the current implementation of the User model for this project:

```python
from application import db
import datetime


__all__ = ['Post']


class Post(db.Model):

    # The unique primary key for each post created.
    id = db.Column(db.Integer, primary_key=True)
    # The free-form text-based content of each post.
    content = db.Column(db.Text())

    #  The date/time that the post was created on.
    created_on = db.Column(db.DateTime(),
        default=datetime.datetime.utcnow, index=True)

    # The user ID that created this post.
    user_id = db.Column(db.Integer(), db.ForeignKey('user.id'))

    def __repr__(self):
        return '<Post %r>' % self.body
```

Once we have our `Post` model defined, we can now add a method to the User model that will allow us to fetch the newsfeed for the user that is linked by the current instance. We name that method `newsfeed`, and it's implementation is as follows:

```python
def newsfeed(self):
    """
    Return all posts from users followed by the current user,
    in descending chronological order.

    """

    join_condition = followers.c.user_id == Post.user_id
    filter_condition = followers.c.follower_id == self.id
    ordering = Post.created_on.desc()

    return Post.query.join(followers,
        (join_condition)).filter(
            filter_condition).order_by(ordering)
```

> Note that we must import the `Post` model to the `application/users/models.py` module in order to implement the preceding method as described. While this particular scenario will function without issue, one must always be wary of the potential circular import problems that may be somewhat difficult to diagnose.

Functional and integration testing

In most of the treatments of unit, functional, and integration testing, it is often recommended that you write the tests before the corresponding code itself is written. While this is generally considered to be a good practice for a variety of reasons (primarily allowing you to ensure that the code being written solves the problem that has been defined), for the sake of simplicity, we have waited until now to touch on this subject.

First, let's create a new `test_settings.py` file that is sibling to our existing `settings.py`. This new file will contain the application configuration constants that we want to use while running our test suite. Most importantly, it will contain the URI to a database that is not our application database, as follows:

```
SQLALCHEMY_DATABASE_URI = 'sqlite:////tmp/test_app.db'
DEBUG = True
TESTING = True
```

 The preceding SQLALCHEMY_DATABASE_URI string points to /tmp/test_app.db as the location for the test database. You may of course choose a different path than the system-wide tmp directory.

We will also make a few additions to the conftest.py file in order to add additional fixtures for initializing a test database and ensuring that we have a SQLAlchemy database session object available for any test functions that may require it:

```python
import pytest
import os
from application import create_app, db as database


DB_LOCATION = '/tmp/test_app.db'


@pytest.fixture(scope='session')
def app():
    app = create_app(config='test_settings')
    return app


@pytest.fixture(scope='session')
def db(app, request):
    """Session-wide test database."""
    if os.path.exists(DB_LOCATION):
        os.unlink(DB_LOCATION)

    database.app = app
    database.create_all()

    def teardown():
        database.drop_all()
        os.unlink(DB_LOCATION)
```

```
        request.addfinalizer(teardown)
        return database



@pytest.fixture(scope='function')
def session(db, request):

        session = db.create_scoped_session()
        db.session = session

        def teardown():
            session.remove()

        request.addfinalizer(teardown)
        return session
```

> The session fixture can be augmented with explicit transactions, ensuring that a transaction is begun and then committed in the teardown. The (simple) implementation of this is left as an exercise to the reader.

The scope argument indicates the lifetime of the given fixture object once it has been created. In the preceding example, we indicated function for the session fixture, which means that a new fixture object will be created for each test function that is invoked as an argument. If we used module as our scope value, we would have a new fixture created for each module that the fixture is included in: a single fixture would be used for all the tests in our module. This should not be confused with the session scope value, which indicates that a single fixture object is to be created for the entire duration of our test suite run. The session scope can be useful in situations where, for example, creating a database connection is an extremely expensive operation. If we only had to create the database connection once, the total runtime of our test suite might be significantly reduced.

For additional information on the scope argument for the py.test fixture decorator and the use of the built-in request object to add the teardown finalizer callback functions, the online documentation is a fantastic starting point: https://pytest.org/latest/contents.html.

We can write a simple test to create a new user from our declarative User model in tests/test_user_model.py:

```
from application.users import models


def test_create_user_instance(session):
    """Create and save a user instance."""

    email = 'test@example.com'
    username = 'test_user'
    password = 'foobarbaz'

    user = models.User(email, username, password)
    session.add(user)
    session.commit()

    # We clear out the database after every run of the test suite
    # but the order of tests may affect which ID is assigned.
    # Let's not depend on magic numbers if we can avoid it.
    assert user.id is not None

    assert user.followed.count() == 0
    assert user.newsfeed().count() == 0
```

After running the test suite with py.test, we should see our newly created test file appear in the listed output and our tests should run without error. We will assert that our newly created user should have an ID (assigned by the database) and should not be following any other users. Consequently, the newsfeed for the user that we created should also have no elements.

Let's add some more tests for the nontrivial parts of our user data model, which will ensure that our follow/following relationships work as expected:

```
def test_user_relationships(session):
    """User following relationships."""

    user_1 = models.User(
        email='test1@example.com', username='test1',
        password='foobarbaz')
    user_2 = models.User(
        email='test2@example.com', username='test2',
```

```
        password='bingbarboo')

    session.add(user_1)
    session.add(user_2)

    session.commit()

    assert user_1.followed.count() == 0
    assert user_2.followed.count() == 0

    user_1.follow(user_2)

    assert user_1.is_following(user_2) is True
    assert user_2.is_following(user_1) is False
    assert user_1.followed.count() == 1

    user_1.unfollow(user_2)

    assert user_1.is_following(user_2) is False
    assert user_1.followed.count() == 0
```

Publish/subscribe events with Blinker

One of the many difficulties in the lifecycle of any nontrivial application is ensuring that the right level of modularity is present in the codebase.

There exist various methodologies to create interfaces, objects, and services and implementing design patterns that help us manage the ever-increasing complexity that is inevitably created for a real-world application. One methodology that is often left unexplored for web applications is the in-process publish-subscribe design pattern.

Generally, publish-subscribe, or more colloquially known as pub/sub, is a messaging pattern where two classes of participants exist: **publishers** and **subscribers**. Publishers send messages and subscribers subscribe to a subset of the messages that are produced via the topic (a named channel) or via the content of the message itself.

In large distributed systems, pub/sub is usually mediated by a message bus or broker that communicates with all the various publishers and subscribers and ensures that the published messages are routed to the subscribers that are interested in them.

For our purpose, however, we can use something a little simpler: an in-process pub/sub system using the wonderfully simple `Blinker` package, which is supported by Flask if it is installed.

Signals from Flask and extensions

When the `Blinker` package is present, Flask allows you to subscribe to various signals (topics) that are published. In addition, Flask extensions may implement their own custom signals. You can subscribe to any number of signals in your application, but the order in which the signal subscribers will receive the messages is undefined.

A few of the more interesting signals that Flask publishes are described in the following list:

- `request_started`: This is sent immediately after the request context was created but before any request processing occurs
- `request_finished`: This is sent after the response has been constructed but immediately before it is sent back to the client

The Flask-SQLAlchemy extension publishes the following two signals itself:

- `models_committed`: This is sent after any modified model instances are committed to the database
- `before_models_committed`: This is sent just before the model instances are committed to the database

Flask-Login publishes half a dozen signals, many of which can be utilized for modularizing the authentication concerns. A few useful ones are listed here:

- `user_logged_in`: This is sent when a user logs in
- `user_logged_out`: This is sent when a user logs out
- `user_unauthorized`: This is sent when an unauthenticated user attempts to access a resource that requires authentication

Creating custom signals

In addition to subscribing to the signal topics that are published by Flask and various Flask extensions, it's also possible (and sometimes very useful!) to create your own custom signals that may then be consumed in your own application. While this may seem like a roundabout approach where a simple function or method call would suffice, the ability to separate out orthogonal concerns from the various parts of your application is an attractive proposal.

For example, say you have a User model that has an `update_password` method, which allows the password for the given user instance to be changed to a new given value. When the password is changed, we would like to send an e-mail to the user, informing them that this action has occurred.

Now, the straightforward implementation of this would be to simply have the mail sent in the `update_password` method itself, which is inherently not a bad idea. Imagine, however, that we have yet another dozen instances where incurred actions require that an e-mail be sent out to the user: when they are followed by a new user, when they are unfollowed by a user, when they reach a certain threshold of followers, and the list goes on.

The problem then becomes apparent: we have mixed logic and functionality to send an e-mail to a user in various parts of our application, which makes it increasingly difficult to reason about, debug, and refactor.

While several methods to manage this complexity exist, the explicit separation of concerns that is possible becomes readily apparent when a publish/subscribe pattern is implemented. With custom signals in our Flask application, we can create a follower-added signal where an event is published after the action takes place and any number of subscribers can listen for that particular event. Moreover, we can organize our application in such a way that the signal subscribers for similar events (for example, sending out an e-mail notification) reside in the same location in the codebase.

Let's create a signal that will publish an event whenever a user follows another user. First, we will need to create our `Namespace` signal container object so that we can then declare our signal topics. Let's do this in `application/__init__.py` module:

```
from flask import Flask
from flask.ext.sqlalchemy import SQLAlchemy
from flask.ext.bcrypt import Bcrypt
from blinker import Namespace


# Initialize the db extension, but without configuring
# it with an application instance.
```

```
db = SQLAlchemy()
flask_bcrypt = Bcrypt()

socializer_signals = Namespace()
user_followed = socializer_signals.signal('user-followed')

# ...
```

Once this is in place, emitting the `user-followed` event in our `User.follow()` method is simple, as follows:

```
def follow(self, user):
    """

    Follow the given user.

    Return `False` if the user was already following the user.
    """

    if self.is_following(user):
        return False
    self.followed.append(user)

    # Publish the signal event using the current model (self) as sender.
    user_followed.send(self)

    return self
```

> Remember to add the `from the application import user_followed` import line at the top of the `application/users/models.py` module.

Once we have an event that is published, a subscriber may be connected. Let's implement the signal handlers in `application/signal_handlers.py`:

```
__all__ = ['user_followed_email']

import logging

logging.basicConfig(level=logging.DEBUG)
logger = logging.getLogger(__name__)
```

```
def user_followed_email(user, **kwargs):
    logger.debug(
        "Send an email to {user}".format(user=user.username))
```

```
from application import user_followed
```

```
def connect_handlers():
    user_followed.connect(user_followed_email)
```

Finally, we will need to ensure that our signal handlers are registered by importing the functions to the application/__init__.py module:

```
from flask import Flask
from flask.ext.sqlalchemy import SQLAlchemy
from flask.ext.bcrypt import Bcrypt
from blinker import Namespace
```

```
# Initialize the db extension, but without configuring
# it with an application instance.
db = SQLAlchemy()
flask_bcrypt = Bcrypt()
```

```
socializer_signals = Namespace()
user_followed = socializer_signals.signal('user-followed')
```

```
from signal_handlers import connect_handlers
connect_handlers()
```

```
# ...
# ...
```

After this is added, every time a user follows another user, we will have a debug message printed to the configured log output. Implementing the functionality to actually send an e-mail to a user is left as an exercise for the reader; a good starting point would be to use the Flask-Mail extension.

Graceful handling of exceptions

No matter how hard we try, sometimes the code that we use and write will raise an exception.

Usually, these exceptions are thrown in, well, exceptional circumstances, but that does not detract from the fact that we should understand which parts of our application may raise an exception and whether or not we want to handle the exception at the point of invocation or simply let it bubble up the call stack to another frame.

For our current application, there are several types of exceptions that we would like to handle in a graceful manner rather than let it crash the entire Python process and bring everything to an ugly, screeching halt.

In the previous chapter, we glossed over some of the necessary exception handling that needs to exist in most Flask and SQLAlchemy-based applications (or nearly any other database abstraction, for that matter), but the importance of handling these exceptions when they do arise cannot be understated. With this in mind, let's create some of the views, forms, and templates that will let us sign up as new users to our application and see a few examples of where and how to handle exceptions when they do arise.

First, let's create our basic user view handlers in `application/users/views.py`:

```python
from flask import Blueprint, render_template, url_for, redirect, flash, g
from flask.ext.login import login_user, logout_user

from flask.ext.wtf import Form
from wtforms import StringField, PasswordField
from wtforms.validators import DataRequired, Length

from models import User
from application import db, flask_bcrypt

users = Blueprint('users', __name__, template_folder='templates')


class Login   Form(Form):
    """
Represents the basic Login form elements & validators.
    """

username = StringField('username',
```

```
        validators=[DataRequired()])
password = PasswordField('password',
        validators=[DataRequired(),Length(min=6)])



class CreateUserForm(Form):
    """

        Encapsulate the necessary information required for creating a
new user.
    """

    username = StringField('username', validators=[DataRequired(),
        Length(min=3, max=40)])
    email = StringField('email', validators=[DataRequired(),
        Length(max=255)])
    password = PasswordField('password', validators=[DataRequired(),
        Length(min=8)])



    @users.route('/signup', methods=['GET', 'POST'])
    def signup():
    """
Basic user creation functionality.

    """

form = CreateUserForm()

if form.validate_on_submit():

        user = User(
          username=form.username.data,
          email=form.email.data,
          password=form.password.data)

        # add the user to the database
        db.session.add(user)
        db.session.commit()
        # Once we have persisted the user to the database successfully,
```

```python
        # authenticate that user for the current session
login_user(user, remember=True)
return redirect(url_for('users.index'))


return render_template('users/signup.html', form=form)



@users.route('/', methods=['GET'])
def index():
return "User index page!", 200



@users.route('/login', methods=['GET', 'POST'])
def login():
    """
Basic user login functionality.

    """

if hasattr(g, 'user') and g.user.is_authenticated():
return redirect(url_for('users.index'))

form = LoginForm()

if form.validate_on_submit():

        # We use one() here instead of first()
    user = User.query.filter_by(username=form.username.data).one()
    if not user or not flask_bcrypt.check_password_hash(user.password,
      form.password.data):

    flash("No such user exists.")
    return render_template('users/login.html', form=form)

    login_user(user, remember=True)
    return redirect(url_for('users.index'))
    return render_template('users/login.html', form=form)



@users.route('/logout', methods=['GET'])
```

```
def logout():
logout_user()
return redirect(url_for('users.login'))
```

You'll notice that much of the login and logout functionality is similar to what we created in the previous chapter using the Flask-Login extension. So, we'll simply include these functionalities and defined routes without comment (in addition to the related Jinja templates) and focus on the new signup route that encapsulates the logic necessary to create a new user. This view utilizes the new `application/users/templates/users/signup.html` view, which simply includes the relevant form controls that allow a user to input their desired username, email address, and password:

```
{% extends "layout.html" %}

{% block content %}

<form action="{{ url_for('users.signup')}}" method="post">
    {{ form.hidden_tag() }}
    {{ form.id }}
    <div>{{ form.username.label }}: {{ form.username }}</div>
    {% if form.username.errors %}
    <ul class="errors">{% for error in form.username.errors %}<li>{{
error }}</li>{% endfor %}</ul>
    {% endif %}

    <div>{{ form.email.label }}: {{ form.email }}</div>
    {% if form.email.errors %}
    <ul class="errors">{% for error in form.email.errors %}<li>{{ error
}}</li>{% endfor %}</ul>
    {% endif %}

    <div>{{ form.password.label }}: {{ form.password }}</div>
    {% if form.password.errors %}
    <ul class="errors">{% for error in form.password.errors %}<li>{{
error }}</li>{% endfor %}</ul>
    {% endif %}

    <div><input type="submit" value="Sign up!"></div>
</form>

{% endblock %}
```

Once we have the preceding template in place, we will update our application factory to bind the user views to the application object. We will also initialize the Flask-Login extension as we did in the previous chapter:

```
from flask import Flask
from flask.ext.sqlalchemy import SQLAlchemy
from flask.ext.bcrypt import Bcrypt
from blinker import Namespace
from flask.ext.login import LoginManager


# Initialize the db extension, but without configuring
# it with an application instance.
db = SQLAlchemy()
flask_bcrypt = Bcrypt()
login_manager = LoginManager()

socializer_signals = Namespace()
user_followed = socializer_signals.signal('user-followed')

from signal_handlers import *


def create_app(config=None):
app = Flask(__name__)

if config is not None:
    app.config.from_object(config)

    # Initialize any extensions and bind blueprints to the
    # application instance here.
    db.init_app(app)
    flask_bcrypt.init_app(app)
    login_manager.init_app(app)

    from application.users.views import users
    app.register_blueprint(users, url_prefix='/users')

    from application.users import models as user_models
    @login_manager.user_loader
```

```
de fload_user(user_id):
    return user_models.User.query.get(int(user_id))


    return app
```

Don't forget to add a SECRET_KEY configuration value to our application/ settings.py module:

```
SQLALCHEMY_DATABASE_URI = 'sqlite:///socializer.db'
SECRET_KEY = 'BpRvzXZ800[-t:=z1eZtx9t/,P*'
```

Now, we should be able to run the application and visit http://localhost:5000/ users/signup, where we will be presented with a series of form inputs to create a new user account. On the successful creation of a new user, we will be automatically authenticated using the login_user() method of the Flask-Login extension.

What we have not accounted for, however, are the situations where the creation of a user fails due to a mismatch with what our SQLAlchemy model and database expect. This may happen for a variety of reasons:

- An existing user has already claimed the submitted value for e-mail or username, both of which have been marked as unique in our user model
- A field requires additional validation criteria specified by the database, which are not met
- The database is unavailable (for example, due to network partition)

In order to ensure that these events are handled in the most graceful manner possible, we must encapsulate the portions of the code that may raise the relevant exceptions that signal one of these conditions. Thus, in our application/users/ views.py module in the signup route, we will modify the portion of the code where we will persist the user to the database:

```
# place with other imports...
from sqlalchemy import exc


# ...


try:
    db.session.add(user)
    db.session.commit()
except exc.IntegrityError as e:
    # A unique column constraint was violated
```

```
current_app.exception("User unique constraint violated.")

return render_template('users/signup.html', form=form)

except exc.SQLAlchemyError:

current_app.exception("Could not save new user!")

flash("Something went wrong while creating this user!")

return render_template('users/signup.html', form=form)
```

Additionally, we will wrap `User.query.filter_by(username=form.username.data).one()` in the login route in the same module with a try/except block, to ensure that we handle the case where the username submitted in the login form does not exist at all in the database:

```
try:
    # We use one() here instead of first()
    user = User.query.filter_by(
            username=form.username.data).one()s
except NoResultFound:
    flash("User {username} does not exist.".format(
        username=form.username.data))
    return render_template('users/login.html', form=form)

# ...
```

Functional testing

Now that we created a few routes and templates to handle user signup and login, let's utilize some of the `py.test` knowledge that we gained earlier in the chapter in order to write some post facto integration tests to ensure that our views are behaving as we expect. First, let's create a new test module in `application/tests/test_user_views.py` and write our first test that uses the client fixture so as to simulate a request to the application via the built-in Werkzeug test client. This will ensure that a proper request context has been constructed so that the context bound objects (for example, `url_for`, g) are available, as follows:

```
def test_get_user_signup_page(client):
    """Ensure signup page is available."""
    response = client.get('/users/signup')
    assert response.status_code == 200
    assert 'Sign up!' in response.data
```

The preceding test first makes a request to the /users/signup route and then asserts that the HTTP response code for this route is 200 (the default value for any successful return render_template() function). Then it asserts that the **Sign up!** button text appears in the returned HTML, which is a relatively safe guarantee that the page in question was rendered without any major errors.

Next, let's add a test for a successful user signup, as follows:

```python
from flask import session, get_flashed_messages
from application.users.models import User
from application import flask_bcrypt


def test_signup_new_user(client):
    """Successfully sign up a new user."""
    data = {'username': 'test_username', 'email': 'test@example.com',
            'password': 'my test password'}

    response = client.post('/users/signup', data=data)

    # On successful creation we redirect.
    assert response.status_code == 302

    # Assert that a session was created due to successful login
    assert '_id' in session

    # Ensure that we have no stored flash messages indicating an error
    # occurred.
    assert get_flashed_messages() == []

    user = User.query.filter_by(username=data['username']).one()

    assert user.email == data['email']
    assert user.password
    assert flask_bcrypt.check_password_hash(
        user.password, data['password'])
```

If we were to run the test suite immediately, it would fail. This is due to a somewhat subtle effect introduced by Flask-WTF, which expects a CSRF token to be provided for any submitted form data. The following are the two ways in which we can fix this:

- We can manually generate a CSRF token in the simulated POST data dictionary; the WTForms library provides the functionality to implement this

- We can set the WTF_CSRF_ENABLED configuration Boolean in the test_ settings.py module to False, so that all the form validations that occur in the test suite will not require a CSRF token in order to be considered valid

The advantage of the first option is that the data sent across the request/response cycle will closely mirror what would happen in a production scenario, with the downside being that we are then responsible for generating (or programmatically abstracting) the required CSRF tokens for every single form that we want to test. The second option allows us to simply stop caring about the CSRF tokens completely while we are in the test suite, which is a downside as well. For the purpose of this chapter, we will use the method outlined in the second option.

In the preceding tests, we will first create a dictionary of our simulated form data that we would like to POST to our signup endpoint and then pass this data to the client. post('/users/signup') method. After the successful signup of a new user, we should expect to be redirected to a different page (we could also check the existence and value of the *Location* header in the response), in addition to the creation of a session ID by Flask-Login that will handle our user sessions. Moreover, a successful signup attempt for our current application means that we should have no flash messages that are stored for display and that a new user record with the provided data should be available and populated with the data that was supplied in the POST.

While most developers are very keen on testing the success path of a request, it's equally, if not more, important to test the most common failure paths. To this end, let's add the following few tests for the most typical failure scenarios, the first of which would be the use of an invalid username:

```python
import pytest
import sqlalchemy


def test_signup_invalid_user(client):
    """Try to sign up with invalid data."""

    data = {'username': 'x', 'email': 'short@example.com',
            'password': 'a great password'}
```

```
    response = client.post('/users/signup', data=data)


    # With a form error, we still return a 200 to the client since
    # browsers are not always the best at handling proper 4xx response
codes.
    assert response.status_code == 200
    assert 'must be between 3 and 40 characters long.' in
response.data
```

 Remember, we defined our form validation rules for user signup in the `application.users.views.CreateUserForm` class; usernames are required to be between 3 and 40 characters long.

```
def test_signup_invalid_user_missing_fields(client):
    """Try to sign up with missing email."""

    data = {'username': 'no_email', 'password': 'a great password'}
    response = client.post('/users/signup', data=data)

    assert response.status_code == 200
    assert 'This field is required' in response.data

    with pytest.raises(sqlalchemy.orm.exc.NoResultFound):
        User.query.filter_by(username=data['username']).one()

    data = {'username': 'no_password', 'email': 'test@example.com'}
    response = client.post('/users/signup', data=data)

    assert response.status_code == 200
    assert 'This field is required' in response.data

    with pytest.raises(sqlalchemy.orm.exc.NoResultFound):
        User.query.filter_by(username=data['username']).one()
```

 In the preceding test, we used an often overlooked convenience function of `py.test` (and other testing libraries), which is the `raises(exc)` context manager. This allows us to wrap a function call where we expect an exception to be raised and will itself cause a failure in the test suite if the expected exception type (or derived type) is not raised.

Your newsfeed

While we have built up most of the supporting architecture to provide the functionality for our Socializer application, we are still missing one of the more fundamental pieces of the puzzle: being able to view the posts of the people you follow in a chronological order.

To make the display of information about the owner of a post a bit simpler, let's add a relationship definition to our `Post` model:

```
class Post(db.Model):
    # ...
    user = db.relationship('User',
        backref=db.backref('posts', lazy='dynamic'))
```

This will allow us to use `post.user` to access any of the user information that is associated with a given post, which is going to be quite useful in any view that displays a single post or a list of posts.

Let's add a route for this in `application/users/views.py`:

```
@users.route('/feed', methods=['GET'])
@login_required
def feed():
    """
    List all posts for the authenticated user; most recent first.
    """
    posts = current_user.newsfeed()
    return render_template('users/feed.html', posts=posts)
```

Note that the preceding snippet uses the `current_user` proxy (which you should import to the module) that is provided by the Flask-Login extension. As the Flask-Login extension stores the user object of the authenticated user in the proxy, we can call methods and attributes on it just as we would on a normal `user` object.

As the previous feed endpoint is up and running, we'll need the supporting template in `application/users/templates/users/feed.html` so that we can actually render a response:

```
{% extends "layout.html" %}


{% block content %}
<div class="new-post">
```

```
    <p><a href="{{url_for('posts.add')}}">New Post</a></p>
  </div>

  {% for post in posts %}
  <div class="post">
    <span class="author">{{post.user.username}}</span>, published on
      <span class="date">{{post.created_on}}</span>
    <pre><code>{{post.content}}</code></pre>
  </div>
  {% endfor %}

  {% endblock %}
```

The last bit that we need is the view handler to add a new post. As we haven't created the `application/posts/views.py` module, let's do that. We'll need a `Flask-WTForm` class to handle/validate the new posts and a route handler to send and process the required fields, all hooked up to a new blueprint:

```python
from flask import Blueprint, render_template, url_for, redirect,
flash, current_app


from flask.ext.login import login_required, current_user

from flask.ext.wtf import Form

from wtforms import StringField

from wtforms.widgets import TextArea

from wtforms.validators import DataRequired

from sqlalchemy import exc


from models import Post

from application import db


posts = Blueprint('posts', __name__, template_folder='templates')



class CreatePostForm(Form):
    """Form for creating new posts."""

    content = StringField('content', widget=TextArea(),
            validators=[DataRequired()])
```

```python
@posts.route('/add', methods=['GET', 'POST'])
@login_required
def add():
    """Add a new post."""

    form = CreatePostForm()
    if form.validate_on_submit():
        user_id = current_user.id

        post = Post(user_id=user_id, content=form.content.data)
        db.session.add(post)

        try:
            db.session.commit()
        except exc.SQLAlchemyError:
            current_app.exception("Could not save new post!")
            flash("Something went wrong while creating your post!")
        else:
            return render_template('posts/add.html', form=form)

    return redirect(url_for('users.feed'))
```

The corresponding `application/posts/templates/posts/add.html` file is, as expected, relatively simple and reminiscent of the view template used in the previous chapter. Here it is:

```html
{% extends "layout.html" %}

{% block content %}
<form action="{{ url_for('posts.add')}}" method="post">

  {{ form.hidden_tag() }}
  {{ form.id }}

  <div class="row">
    <div>{{ form.content.label }}: {{ form.content }}</div>
    {% if form.content.errors %}
    <ul class="errors">{% for error in form.content.errors
      %}<li>{{ error }}</li>{% endfor %}</ul>
    {% endif %}
  </div>
```

```
    <div><input type="submit" value="Post"></div>
</form>

{% endblock %}
```

Finally, we will need to make the application aware of this newly created posts blueprint by binding it to our application object in our application factory, in application/__init__.py:

```
def create_app(config=None):
    app = Flask(__name__)

    # …
    from application.users.views import users
    app.register_blueprint(users, url_prefix='/users')

    from application.posts.views import posts
    app.register_blueprint(posts, url_prefix='/posts')

        # …
```

Once the preceding code is in place, we can generate a few test users and posts for these users by creating user accounts via the web interface at the /users/signup endpoint and then creating posts for the users at /posts/add. Otherwise, we could create a small CLI script to do this for us, which we will learn how to implement in the next chapter. We could also write a few test cases to ensure that the newsfeed works as expected. Actually, we could do all three!

Summary

We started this chapter by first introducing the concept of an application factory and described some of the benefits and trade-offs of this approach. Next, we used our newly created application factory to set up our first test suite using py.test, which required some modification as to how our application object was created in order to ensure that we obtained a suitable instance that was configured to test scenarios.

Then, we dove headfirst into implementing the basic data models behind a typical web application that contained *social* features with the ability to follow other users and be followed ourselves. We briefly touched on several main implementation patterns for so-called newsfeed applications and used the simplest version for our own data models.

This then led us to discuss and explore the concept of the publish/subscribe design pattern, of which an in-process implementation can be found in the `Blinker` package that Flask and various Flask extensions integrate. Using this new knowledge, we created our own publishers and subscribers, allowing us to address some common cross-cutting concerns that exist in many modern web applications.

For our next project, we will switch gears from creating the HTML-based forms and views that we have used for the past few chapters and focus on another very important part of modern web applications: providing a useful JSON API to interact with.

5
Shutterbug, the Photo Stream API

In this chapter, we will build a (primarily) JSON-based API that allows us to view a reverse chronologically ordered list of photos that have been added – this has become quite popular in recent years due to Instagram and similar photo sharing applications. For the sake of simplicity, we will forgo the usual social aspect that many of these applications are typically built around; however, you are encouraged to combine the knowledge of the previous chapters with the information in this chapter to build such an application.

Shutterbug, the minimal API-only application that we are about to embark on, will allow a user to upload a photograph of their choosing via an authenticated, JSON-based API.

Additionally, we will use one of the lesser-known features of Flask (Werkzeug, really) to create a custom middleware that will allow us to intercept inbound requests and modify the global application environment for very simple API versioning.

Starting off
Once more, as we did in the previous chapters, let's create a completely new directory and virtual environment for this application:

```
$ mkdir -p ~/src/shutterbug && cd ~/src/shutterbug
$ mkvirtualenv shutterbug
$ pip install flask flask-sqlalchemy pytest-flask flask-bcrypt
```

Create the following application layout to start:

```
├── application/
│   ├── __init__.py
│   └── resources
│       ├── __init__.py
│       └── photos.py
├── conftest.py
├── database.py
├── run.py
├── settings.py
└── tests/
```

> The application layout presented here is different from the typical Blueprint-based structure that we used in previous chapters; we will use the suggested layout for typical Flask-RESTful applications, which also suits the simplicity of the Shutterbug application.

The application factory

We will use the application factory pattern again in this chapter; let's add our skeleton `create_app` method to the `application/__init__.py` module and include our Flask-SQLAlchemy database initialization as well:

```python
from flask import Flask
from flask.ext.sqlalchemy import SQLAlchemy
from flask.ext.bcrypt import Bcrypt


# Initialize the db extension, but without configuring
# it with an application instance.
db = SQLAlchemy()
flask_bcrypt = Bcrypt()


def create_app(config=None):
    app = Flask(__name__)

    if config is not None:
```

```
    app.config.from_object(config)

    db.init_app(app)
    flask_bcrypt.init_app(app)

    return app
```

Let's include our barebones `run.py`:

```
from application import create_app

app = create_app()
app.run()
```

This should give us the ability to run the application using the built-in Werkzeug application server via the following code:

```
$ python run.py
```

Interlude – Werkzeug

We've spoken about Werkzeug a few times during the course of this book but we haven't really explained what it is, why we use it, or why it's useful. To understand Werkzeug, we first need to know why it exists. For this, we will need to understand the origins of the Python Web Server Gateway Interface specification, most commonly abbreviated as WSGI.

Today, choosing a Python web application framework is a relatively simple matter of preference: most developers choose a framework based on a previous experience, necessity (for example, one that is designed for an asynchronous request processing such as Tornado), or some other quantifiable or unquantifiable criteria.

Several years ago, however, the choice of an application framework affected the web server that you could use. As all Python web application frameworks at the time implemented their own HTTP request processing in a slightly different manner, they were often only compatible with a subset of web servers. Developers, tired of this somewhat inconvenient status quo, put forth a proposal to unify the interaction of web servers with Python applications through a common specification, WSGI.

The WSGI specification, once established, was adopted by all the major frameworks. Additionally, several so-called *utility* tools were created; they had the sole purpose of bridging the official WSGI specification, which can be somewhat unfriendly to work with for new developers, with a more robust intermediate API that aided the development of modern web applications. Moreover, these utility libraries could then be used as the foundation for more feature-complete and robust application frameworks.

As you may have guessed by now, Werkzeug is one of these WSGI utility libraries. When combined with Jinja, the templating language, and some convenient defaults for configuration, routing, and other basic web application necessities, we have Flask.

Flask is what we primarily deal with in this book, but a fairly large part of the hard work abstracted away from you is contained in Werkzeug. While it largely goes unnoticed, it is possible to interact with it directly in order to intercept and modify portions of a request before Flask has the chance to process it. We'll explore some of these possibilities later on in the chapter when we implement a custom Werkzeug middleware for optionally versioning JSON API requests.

Simple APIs with Flask-RESTful

One of the great joys of using Flask is the seemingly infinite extensibility and composability that it offers. As it's a rather thin layer that sits atop Werkzeug and Jinja, it does not impose much on the developer in terms of constraints.

Due to this flexibility, we have extensions such as Flask-RESTful at our disposal, which make creating JSON-based APIs a joy. First, let's install the package:

```
$ pip install flask-restful
```

Next, let's initialize the extension in our application factory in the usual fashion:

```
from flask import Flask
from flask.ext.sqlalchemy import SQLAlchemy
from flask.ext.bcrypt import Bcrypt
from flask.ext.restful import Api

# .........
api = Api()

def create_app(config=None):
    app = Flask(__name__)

    if config is not None:
        app.config.from_object(config)

    db.init_app(app)
    flask_bcrypt.init_app(app)

    api.init_app(app)

    return app
```

The primary building block of the Flask-RESTful extension is the concept of a resource. A resource is, for all intents and purposes, a `Flask` method view with some very useful defaults set for content-type negotiation. If you haven't encountered the concept of a `MethodView` in Flask until now, don't fret! They're quite straightforward and provide you with a relatively simple interface to separate the RESTful resources by allowing you to define methods on a class that maps directly to the basic HTTP verbs: `GET`, `PUT`, `POST`, `PATCH`, and `DELETE`. The Flask-RESTful resource, in turn, extends the `MethodView` class and thus allows for the same style of verb-based route handling.

More concretely, it means that the Flask-RESTful API nouns can be written in the following way. We will first add our photo resource view handlers to `application/resources/photos.py`:

```python
class SinglePhoto(Resource):

    def get(self, photo_id):
        """Handling of GET requests."""
        pass

    def delete(self, photo_id):
        """Handling of DELETE requests."""
        pass


class ListPhoto(Resource):

    def get(self):
        """Handling of GET requests."""
        pass

    def post(self):
        """Handling of POST requests."""
        pass
```

> In the preceding two `Resource` subclasses, we defined a subset of the HTTP verbs that are possible to handle; we are not required to define handlers for all the possible verbs. If, for example, our application were to receive a PATCH request to one of the preceding resources, Flask would return an HTTP/1.1 405 Method Not Allowed.

Then, we will import these view handlers to our application factory in
application/__init__.py in order to bind these two classes to our
Flask-RESTful API object:

```
from flask import Flask
from flask.ext.sqlalchemy import SQLAlchemy
from flask.ext.restful import Api
from flask.ext.bcrypt import Bcrypt

# Initialize the db extension, but without configuring
# it with an application instance.
db = SQLAlchemy()
api = Api()
flask_bcrypt = Bcrypt()



def create_app(config=None):
    app = Flask(__name__)

    if config is not None:
        app.config.from_object(config)

    db.init_app(app)
    flask_bcrypt.init_app(app)


    from .resources.photos import SinglePhoto, ListPhoto
    api.add_resource(ListPhoto, '/photos')
    api.add_resource(SinglePhoto, '/photos/<int:photo_id>')

    api.init_app(app)

    return app
```

 Note that we have bound the resources to the API object
before we call api.init_app(app). If we initialize before
we bind the resources, the routes will not exist on the Flask
application object.

We can confirm that the routes we defined are mapped to the application object by
starting an interactive Python session and checking the url_map attribute of our
Flask application

Start the session from the parent of the application folder so that the `PYTHONPATH` is set correctly:

```
In [1]: from application import create_app
In [2]: app = create_app()
In [3]: app.url_map
Out[3]:
Map([<Rule '/photos' (HEAD, POST, OPTIONS, GET) -> listphoto>,
 <Rule '/photos/<photo_id>' (HEAD, DELETE, OPTIONS, GET) -> singlephoto>,
 <Rule '/static/<filename>' (HEAD, OPTIONS, GET) -> static>])
```

The preceding output lists a Werkzeug `Map` object, which contains three `Rule` objects, each of which lists a URI, the HTTP verbs that are valid against this URI, and a normalized identifier (as view handlers can be functions as well as `MethodView` subclasses in addition to a few other options) that indicates which view handler will be invoked.

 Flask will automatically handle the HEAD and OPTIONS verbs for all the defined endpoints and also add a default /`static/<filename>` route for the static file handling. This default static route can be disabled, if necessary, by setting the `static_folder` argument to the `Flask` object initialization in our application factory to None:

```
app = Flask(__name__, static_folder=None)
```

Let's do the same thing for our skeleton user view resource handlers, which we will declare in `application/resources/users.py`:

```python
from flask.ext.restful import Resource


class SingleUser(Resource):

    def get(self, user_id):
        """Handling of GET requests."""
        pass


class CreateUser(Resource):

    def post(self):
        """Handling of POST requests."""
        pass
```

Note that we could have put the `post` method handler on the `SingleUser` resource definition but instead, we split it out to its own resource. This is not strictly necessary but will make things a bit easier to follow for our application and only cost us a few extra lines of code.

Similar to what we did with our photo views, we'll add them to our Flask-RESTful API object in our application factory:

```
def create_app(config=None):

    # …

    from .resources.photos import SinglePhoto, ListPhoto
    from .resources.users import SingleUser, CreateUser

    api.add_resource(ListPhoto, '/photos')
    api.add_resource(SinglePhoto, '/photos/<int:photo_id>')
    api.add_resource(SingleUser, '/users/<int:user_id>')
    api.add_resource(CreateUser, '/users')

    api.init_app(app)
    return app
```

Improved password handling with hybrid attributes

Our `User` model will be quite similar to the one that we used in the previous chapter and will use a class attribute `getter`/`setter` for the `password` attribute. This will ensure a consistent application of the Bcrypt key derivation function to the raw user password regardless of whether we set the value at the time of object creation or manually set the attribute of an already created object.

This consists of using the `hybrid_property` descriptor from SQLAlchemy, which allows us to define properties that act differently when accessed at the class-level (for example, `User.password`, where we want the SQL expression for the password field of the user model to be returned) versus instance-level (for example, `User().password`, where we want the actual encrypted password string of a user object to be returned instead of the SQL expression).

We will define the password class attribute as `_password`, which will ensure that we avoid any nasty attribute/method name collisions, so that we can define the hybrid `getter` and `setter` methods correctly.

As our application will be relatively simple in terms of data modeling, we can use a single module for our models in `application/models.py`:

```python
from application import db, flask_bcrypt
from sqlalchemy.ext.hybrid import hybrid_property

import datetime

class User(db.Model):
    """SQLAlchemy User model."""

    # The primary key for each user record.
    id = db.Column(db.Integer, primary_key=True)

    # The unique email for each user record.
    email = db.Column(db.String(255), unique=True, nullable=False)

    # The unique username for each record.
    username = db.Column(db.String(40), unique=True, nullable=False)

    # The bcrypt'ed user password
    _password = db.Column('password', db.String(60), nullable=False)

    #  The date/time that the user account was created on.
    created_on = db.Column(db.DateTime,
        default=datetime.datetime.utcnow)

    def __repr__(self):
        return '<User %r>' % self.username

    @hybrid_property
    def password(self):
        """The bcrypt'ed password of the given user."""

        return self._password

    @password.setter
    def password(self, password):
        """Bcrypt the password on assignment."""

        self._password = flask_bcrypt.generate_password_hash(password)
```

In the same module, we can then declare our `Photo` model, which will be charged with maintaining all the metadata related to an image but not the image itself:

```python
class Photo(db.Model):
    """SQLAlchemy Photo model."""

    # The unique primary key for each photo created.
    id = db.Column(db.Integer, primary_key=True)

    # The free-form text-based comment of each photo.
    comment = db.Column(db.Text())

    # Path to photo on local disk
    path = db.Column(db.String(255), nullable=False)

    #  The date/time that the photo was created on.
    created_on = db.Column(db.DateTime(),
        default=datetime.datetime.utcnow, index=True)

    # The user ID that created this photo.
    user_id = db.Column(db.Integer(), db.ForeignKey('user.id'))

    # The attribute reference for accessing photos posted by this
user.
    user = db.relationship('User', backref=db.backref('photos',
        lazy='dynamic'))

    def __repr__(self):
        return '<Photo %r>' % self.comment
```

API authentication

For most applications and APIs, the concepts of authentication and authorization are central to nontrivial operations:

- **Authentication**: This asserts the veracity of the credentials provided and also ensures that they belong to a known entity; in simple terms, this means ensuring that the username and password provided to an application belong to a valid user. Once verified, the application assumes that the requests performed with these credentials are being performed on behalf of the given user.

- **Authorization**: These are the permissible actions of an authenticated (or unauthenticated) entity in the bounds of the application. In most situations, authorization presupposes that a pre-existing authentication step was performed. An entity may be authenticated but not authorized to access certain resources: if you enter your card and PIN in an ATM (thus authenticating yourself), you can view your own accounts, but attempting to view the accounts of another person will (hopefully!) result in a refusal as you are not authorized to access that information.

For Shutterbug, we are only concerned with authentication. If we were to add various features that included, say, the ability to create private groups of users that have access to a shared pool of photos, then systematized authorization would be required to determine which users can access which subsets of resources.

Authentication protocols

Many developers will already be familiar with several authentication protocols: the usual identifier/password combination that is standard across most web applications in existence and OAuth for many modern APIs (for example, Twitter, Facebook, GitHub, and others). For our own application, we will use the incredibly simple HTTP Basic authentication protocol.

While HTTP Basic is not the most flexible nor secure (it provides no encryption whatsoever, actually), it is reasonable to implement this protocol for simple applications, demos, and prototype APIs. In the early days of Twitter, it was actually the only method by which you could authenticate with their API! Moreover, when transmitting data over HTTPS, which we should do in any production-level environment, we are assured that the plaintext request that includes our user identifier and password is encrypted from any malicious third parties that may be listening in.

The implementation of the HTTP Basic authentication is not overly complex, but it's most definitely something that we can offload to an extension. Let's go ahead and install Flask-HTTPAuth to our environment, which consists of creating an instance of the extension:

```
$ pip install flask-httpauth
```

And set up the extension in our application/__init__.py:

```
from flask import Flask
from flask.ext.sqlalchemy import SQLAlchemy
from flask.ext.restful import Api
from flask.ext.bcrypt import Bcrypt
from flask.ext.httpauth import HTTPBasicAuth
```

```
# …

api = Api()
flask_bcrypt = Bcrypt()
auth = HTTPBasicAuth()

def create_app(config=None):
    # …

    import authentication

    api.add_resource(ListPhoto, '/photos')
    api.add_resource(SinglePhoto, '/photos/<int:photo_id>')

    # …
```

Flask-HTTPAuth includes various decorators to declare handlers/callbacks in order
to perform parts of the authentication process. We'll implement the one that gives
us the most control over how the authentication is performed and put this in a new
module in application/authentication.py. In addition to the verification of the
credentials, we will attach the SQLAlchemy user object to the Flask context local g on
successful authentication so that we can utilize this data in other parts of the request
processing and response generation:

```
import sqlalchemy
from . import auth, flask_bcrypt
from .models import User
from flask import g


@auth.verify_password
def verify_password(username, password):
    """Verify a username/hashed password tuple."""

    try:
        user = User.query.filter_by(username=username).one()
    except sqlalchemy.orm.exc.NoResultFound:
        # We found no username that matched
        return False

    # Perform password hash comparison in time-constant manner.
    verified = flask_bcrypt.check_password_hash(user.password,
        password)
```

```
    if verified is True:
        g.current_user = user

    return verified
```

The `auth.verify_password` decorator allows us to specify a function that accepts a username and password, both of which are extracted out of the Authorization header that is sent with the request. We will then use this information to query our database for a user with the same username, and upon successfully finding one, we will ensure that the provided password hashes to the same value that we stored for this user. If the password does not match or the username does not exist, we will return False and Flask-HTTPAuth will return a 401 Unauthorized header to the requesting client.

Now, to actually use the HTTP Basic authentication, we need to add the `auth.login_required` decorator to the view handlers that will require authentication. We know that all user operations (except creating a new user) will require an authenticated request, so let's implement this:

```
from flask.ext.restful import Resource
from application import auth


class SingleUser(Resource):

    method_decorators = [auth.login_required]

    def get(self, user_id):
        """Handling of GET requests."""
        pass

    # ...
```

> Due to the fact that the self argument for a method of a Resource object refers to the Resource instance and not the method, we cannot use regular view decorators on the individual methods of the view. Rather, we must use the `method_decorators` class attribute, which will apply the declared functions (in order!) to the view method that has been invoked to handle the request.

Getting users

Now that we've figured out the authentication portion of the application, let's implement the API endpoints to create a new user and fetch the existing user data. We can flesh out the get() method of the SingleUser resource class as follows:

```python
from flask.ext.restful import abort

# ...

def get(self, user_id):
    """Handling of GET requests."""

    if g.current_user.id != user_id:
        # A user may only access their own user data.
        abort(403, message="You have insufficient permissions"
            " to access this resource.")

    # We could simply use the `current_user`,
    # but the SQLAlchemy identity map makes this a virtual
    # no-op and alos allows for future expansion
    # when users may access information of other users
    try:
        user = User.query.filter(User.id == user_id).one()
    except sqlalchemy.orm.exc.NoResultFound:
        abort(404, message="No such user exists!")

    data = dict(
        id=user.id,
        username=user.username,
        email=user.email,
        created_on=user.created_on)

    return data, 200
```

There are quite a few new things happening in the preceding method, so let's deconstruct it. First, we will check that the user_id specified in the request (for example, GET /users/1) is the same as the currently authenticated user:

```python
if g.current_user.id != user_id:
        # A user may only access their own user data.
        abort(403, message="You have insufficient permissions"
            " to access this resource.")
```

While this may seem redundant at the moment, it plays a dual role in allowing simpler future modifications to the authorization scheme in addition to adhering to a somewhat more RESTful approach. Here, a resource is uniquely specified by its URI, which is constructed in part by the unique primary key identifier of a user object.

After the authorization check, we will pull the relevant user out of the database by querying it via the `user_id` parameter passed as a named URI parameter:

```
try:
    user = User.query.filter(User.id == user_id).one()
except sqlalchemy.orm.exc.NoResultFound:
    abort(404, message="No such user exists!")
```

If no such user is found, then we will abort the current request with an HTTP 404 Not Found and specify a message in order to make the reason for the non-20x response more clear.

Finally, we will construct a dictionary of the user data that we want to return as a response. We clearly don't want to return the hashed password or other sensitive information, so we will explicitly specify which fields we want to be serialized in the response:

```
data = dict(id=user.id, username=user.username, email=user.email,
            created_on=user.created_on)


    return data, 200
```

Thanks to Flask-RESTful, we do not need to explicitly convert our dictionary to a JSON string: The response representation is `application/json` by default. There's one small catch, however: the JSON encoder that Flask-RESTful uses as a default does not know how to convert Python `datetime` objects to their RFC822 string representations. This can be fixed by specifying the `application/json` MIME type representation handler and ensuring that we use the `flask.json` encoder instead of the default `json` module from the Python standard library.

We can add the following to our `application/__init__.py` module:

```
from flask import Flask, json, make_response
from flask.ext.sqlalchemy import SQLAlchemy
from flask.ext.restful import Api
from flask.ext.bcrypt import Bcrypt
from flask.ext.httpauth import HTTPBasicAuth

# ...

db = SQLAlchemy()
```

```
# ...


@api.representation('application/json')
def output_json(data, code, headers=None):
    resp = make_response(json.dumps(data), code)
    resp.headers.extend(headers or {})
    return resp
```

Creating new users

The analog to fetch the existing users from the API is, of course, to create new users. While typical web applications do this with a signup process that has you fill out various form fields, creating a new user via our API requires that the information be submitted to the server via a POST request, validated, and then a new user is inserted in the database. The implementation of these steps should be put in the post() method of our CreateUser resource:

```
class CreateUser(Resource):

    def post(self):
        """Create a new user."""

        data = request.json
        user = User(**data)

        db.session.add(user)

        try:
            db.session.commit()
        except sqlalchemy.exc.IntegrityError:
            abort(409, message="User already exists!")

        data = dict(id=user.id, username=user.username,
            email=user.email, created_on=user.created_on)

        return data, 201, {'Location': url_for(
            'singleuser', user_id=user.id, _external=True)}
```

 The request.json file is populated with the POST data if, and only if, the content-type of the request is set to application/json.

There's nothing too surprising in the preceding method implementation: we fetched the POST data from `request.json`, created a `User` object (Very insecurely! You can see a bit later on in this chapter for a better alternative.) from it, attempted to add it to the database and catch the exception raised if a user of the same username or e-mail address already exists, and then serialized an HTTP 201 Created response with a `Location` header that includes the URI of the newly created user.

Input validation

While Flask includes a relatively simple way of accessing the POST'ed data via the `flask.request` proxy object, it does not contain any functionality to validate that the data is formatted as we expect it to be. This is okay! Flask attempts to be as agnostic as possible with regards to the data storage and manipulation, leaving this to the developer. Luckily for us, Flask-RESTful includes the `reqparse` module that can be used for the data validation and its usage is very similar in spirit to the popular `argparse` library used for CLI argument parsing.

We will set up our new user data parser/validator in our `application/resources/users.py` module and declare our fields and their types and whether they are required in the POST data to be considered as valid requests or not:

```
from flask.ext.restful import Resource, abort, reqparse, url_for

# …

new_user_parser = reqparse.RequestParser()
new_user_parser.add_argument('username', type=str, required=True)
new_user_parser.add_argument('email', type=str, required=True)
new_user_parser.add_argument('password', type=str, required=True)
```

Now that we have the `new_user_parser` setup in our module, we can modify the `CreateUser.post()` method to utilize this instead:

```
def post(self):
    """Handling of POST requests."""

    data = new_user_parser.parse_args(strict=True)
    user = User(**data)

    db.session.add(user)

    # …
```

The `new_user_parser.parse_args(strict=True)` invocation will attempt to match the declared types and requirements for the fields that we defined via `add_argument` earlier and will internally `abort()` with an HTTP 400 error in case any fields do not pass validation or there are additional fields in the request that we have not explicitly accounted for. (Thanks to the `strict=True` option.)

The use of `reqparse` to validate the POST'ed data can be more cumbersome than the direct assignment that we had previously, but is more secure by an order of magnitude. With the direct assignment technique a malicious user might send arbitrary data in the hope of overriding fields that they should not have access to. For example, our database could contain the internal only `subscription_exipires_on` `datetime` field and a nefarious user could then submit a POST request containing a value for this field set to the far future. Definitely something that we'd like to avoid!

API testing

Let's apply some of the knowledge that we gained in the previous chapters with regards to functional and integration testing with `pytest`.

Our first step (after the requisite pip install `pytest-flask`, of course) is to add a `conftest.py` file as we did in the previous chapters, which is sibling to our `application/` folder:

```python
import pytest
import os
from application import create_app, db as database

DB_LOCATION = '/tmp/test_shutterbug.db'


@pytest.fixture(scope='session')
def app():
    app = create_app(config='test_settings')
    return app


@pytest.fixture(scope='function')
def db(app, request):
    """Session-wide test database."""
    if os.path.exists(DB_LOCATION):
        os.unlink(DB_LOCATION)

    database.app = app
    database.create_all()
```

```
def teardown():
    database.drop_all()
    os.unlink(DB_LOCATION)

request.addfinalizer(teardown)
return database


@pytest.fixture(scope='function')
def session(db, request):

    session = db.create_scoped_session()
    db.session = session

    def teardown():
        session.remove()

    request.addfinalizer(teardown)
    return session
```

The preceding conftest.py file contains the basic test fixtures that we will need in order to write our API tests properly; there should be no surprises here. We will then add our test_settings.py file, which is sibling to the newly created conftest.py, and populate it with the application configuration values that we want for our test runs:

```
SQLALCHEMY_DATABASE_URI = 'sqlite://///tmp/test_shutterbug.db'
SECRET_KEY = b"\x98\x9e\xbaP'D\x03\xf5\x91u5G\x1f"
DEBUG = True
UPLOAD_FOLDER = '/tmp/'
TESTING = True
```

Once this is in place, we can begin writing our test functions and assertions in tests/test_users.py. Our first test will ensure that we can create a new user via the API and the URI of the newly created resource is returned to us in the Location header:

```
from application.models import User
from flask import json
import base64


def test_create_new_user(db, session, client):
    """Attempt to create a basic user."""
```

```
data = {'username': 'you', 'email': 'you@example.com',
        'password': 'foobar'}

response = client.post('/users', data=data)
assert response.status_code == 201
assert 'Location' in response.headers

user = User.query.filter(User.username == data['username']).one()

assert '/users/{}'.format(user.id) in response.headers['Location']
```

Once we've established that a user can be created, the next logical step is to test that an error is returned if a client attempts to create a user with invalid or missing parameters:

```
def test_create_invalid_user(db, session, client):
    """Try to create a user with invalid/missing information."""

    data = {'email': 'you@example.com'}
    response = client.post('/users', data=data)

    assert response.status_code == 400
    assert 'message' in response.json
    assert 'username' in response.json['message']
```

As a sanity check for our HTTP Basic authentication implementation, let's also add a test to fetch a single user record, which requires the request to be authenticated:

```
def test_get_single_user_authenticated(db, session, client):
    """Attempt to fetch a user."""

    data = {'username': 'authed', 'email': 'authed@example.com',
            'password': 'foobar'}
    user = User(**data)
    session.add(user)
    session.commit()

    creds = base64.b64encode(
        b'{0}:{1}'.format(
            user.username, data['password'])).decode('utf-8')

    response = client.get('/users/{}'.format(user.id),
        headers={'Authorization': 'Basic ' + creds})

    assert response.status_code == 200
    assert json.loads(response.get_data())['id'] == user.id
```

The associated test for an unauthenticated request for a single user record is as follows:

```
def test_get_single_user_unauthenticated(db, session, client):
    data = {'username': 'authed', 'email': 'authed@example.com',
            'password': 'foobar'}
    user = User(**data)
    session.add(user)
    session.commit()

    response = client.get('/users/{}'.format(user.id))
    assert response.status_code == 401
```

We can also test that our very simple authorization implementation functions as expected (Recall that we only allow authenticated users to view their own information and not that of any other users in the system.) with a test that creates two users and attempts to access each other's data via authenticated requests:

```
def test_get_single_user_unauthorized(db, session, client):

    alice_data = {'username': 'alice', 'email': 'alice@example.com',
            'password': 'foobar'}
    bob_data = {'username': 'bob', 'email': 'bob@example.com',
            'password': 'foobar'}
    alice = User(**alice_data)
    bob = User(**bob_data)

    session.add(alice)
    session.add(bob)

    session.commit()

    alice_creds = base64.b64encode(b'{0}:{1}'.format(
        alice.username, alice_data['password'])).decode('utf-8')

    bob_creds = base64.b64encode(b'{0}:{1}'.format(
        bob.username, bob_data['password'])).decode('utf-8')

    response = client.get('/users/{}'.format(alice.id),
        headers={'Authorization': 'Basic ' + bob_creds})

    assert response.status_code == 403

    response = client.get('/users/{}'.format(bob.id),
        headers={'Authorization': 'Basic ' + alice_creds})

    assert response.status_code == 403
```

Interlude – Werkzeug middlewares

For certain tasks, we sometimes need the ability to modify the inbound request data and/or environment before the request is routed to a handler function or method. In many situations, the easiest way to achieve this would be to register a function with the `before_request` decorator; this is often used to set `request-global` values on the `g` object or create a database connection.

While this should suffice for a large portion of the most common use cases, sometimes it's more convenient to drop down below the Flask application object (when the request proxy object is constructed) but above the HTTP server. For this, we have the concept of middlewares. Additionally, a properly written middleware will be portable across other compatible WSGI implementations; there's nothing stopping you (barring any application-specific oddities) from using a middleware originally written for a Django application in our current Flask application.

Middlewares are relatively simple things: they are essentially any callable (classes, instances, functions, or methods that can be invoked in a manner similar to a function) that return the proper response format so that the other middlewares in the chain can be invoked correctly.

One example of a middleware that is useful for our current API-based application is one that allows us to extract an optional version number from the request URIs and store this information in the environment so that it can be used at various points during the request processing. For example, a request to `/v0.1a/users/2` will be routed to the handler for `/users/2` and `v0.1a` will be accessible via `request.environ['API_VERSION']` in the Flask application itself.

In a new module in `application/middlewares.py`, we can implement it as follows:

```python
import re

version_pattern = re.compile(r"/v(?P<version>[0-9a-z\-\+\.]+)",
re.IGNORECASE)

class VersionedAPIMiddleware(object):
    """

    The line wrapping here is a bit off, but it's not critical.

    """

    def __init__(self, app):
        self.app = app
```

```
def __call__(self, environ, start_response):
    path = environ.get('PATH_INFO', '')

    match = version_pattern.match(path)

    if match:
        environ['API_VERSION'] = match.group(1)
        environ['PATH_INFO'] = re.sub(version_pattern, '', path,
            count=1)
    else:
        environ['API_VERSION'] = None

    return self.app(environ, start_response)
```

We will bind this middleware to the application object in our factory:

```
# …

from .middlewares import VersionedAPIMiddleware

# …
def create_app(config=None):
    app = Flask(__name__, static_folder=None)
    app.wsgi_app = VersionedAPIMiddleware(app.wsgi_app)

    # …

    api.init_app(app)
    return app
```

 When adding multiple WSGI middlewares, their order can sometimes matter. Be sure to keep this in mind when adding middlewares that can modify the WSGI environment.

Once bound, the middleware is inserted into the request processing before Flask receives the request even though we clearly instantiated a Flask application object. Accessing the API_VERSION value in your application is a simple matter of querying the key bound to the request environment:

```
from flask import request
# …
# …
if request.environ['API_VERSION'] > 2:
    # Handle this differently
else:
    # Handle it normally
```

The parsing of the API version numbers could also be extended to examining the HTTP headers (custom or otherwise) in addition to the URL-based version extraction that we have provided here; a case could be made for the convenience of either.

Back to Shutterbug – uploading photos

Now that we have a minimal but functional API to create and fetch users, we need a similar one to upload photos. First, we will use the same resource pattern that we used previously in addition to defining a RequestParser instance to validate the user submitted data regarding the photos:

```
from flask.ext.restful import Resource, reqparse
from flask import current_app, request, g, url_for
from application import auth, db, models
import uuid
import os
import werkzeug


new_photo_parser = reqparse.RequestParser()
new_photo_parser.add_argument('comment', type=str,
    required=False)
new_photo_parser.add_argument('photo',
    type=werkzeug.datastructures.FileStorage,
    required=True, location='files')


class UploadPhoto(Resource):

    method_decorators = [auth.login_required]

    def post(self):
        """Adds a new photo via form-encoded POST data."""
```

```
data = new_photo_parser.parse_args(strict=True)

# Save our file to the filesystem first
f = request.files['photo']

extension = os.path.splitext(f.filename)[1]
name = werkzeug.utils.secure_filename(
    str(uuid.uuid4()) + extension)
path = os.path.join(
    current_app.config['UPLOAD_FOLDER'], name)

f.save(path)

data['user_id'] = g.current_user.id
data['path'] = path

# Get rid of the binary data that was sent; we've already
# saved this to disk.
del data['photo']

# Add a new Photo entry to the database once we have
# successfully saved the file to the filesystem above.
photo = models.Photo(**data)
db.session.add(photo)
db.session.commit()

data = dict(id=photo.id,
    path=photo.path, comment=photo.comment,
    created_on=photo.created_on)

return data, 201, {'Location': url_for('singlephoto',
    photo_id=photo.id, _external=True)}
```

Note that in the preceding `UploadPhoto` resource, we are accessing `request.files` to extract the binary data that was POST'ed to the endpoint. We then parsed out the extension, generated a unique random string to act as the filename, and finally saved the file to a known UPLOAD_FOLDER that we configured in our application configuration.

Note that we used the `werkzeug.utils.secure_filename` function to sanitize the extension of the uploaded image in order to ensure that it is not vulnerable to path traversal or other filesystem-based exploits that are common when dealing with user uploaded binary data.

There are many other verifications and sanitization steps (for example, ensuring that the MIME type of the file matches the extension and binary data that was actually uploaded, limiting the size/dimensions of the image) that should be performed when accepting untrusted data that will be persisted to a filesystem, but we omit them for the sake of brevity. Data validation techniques and best practices could fill an entire book in themselves.

The local filesystem path that we end up persisting the image to is then added to our photo SQLAlchemy record along with the optional comment that may have accompanied the photo upload. The whole lot is then added to the session and committed to the database before returning a 201 response with the location of the newly created asset in the headers. There are some simple error conditions that we avoid handling in this so that we can focus on the core concepts presented and their implementation is left as an exercise for the reader.

Before taking any of the new photo upload functionalities out for a spin, make sure to bind the resource to the API object in our application factory:

```
def create_app(config=None):
    # …

    from .resources.photos import (SinglePhoto, ListPhoto,
        UploadPhoto)
    # …

    api.add_resource(ListPhoto, '/photos')
    api.add_resource(UploadPhoto, '/photos')
    api.add_resource(SinglePhoto, '/photos/<int:photo_id>')
    api.add_resource(SingleUser, '/users/<int:user_id>')
    api.add_resource(CreateUser, '/users')


    # …
```

File uploads in distributed systems

We have greatly simplified the treatment of file uploads in modern web applications. Of course, simplicity often has several downsides.

The most glaring of these is that in the preceding implementation, we are restricted to a single application server. If multiple application servers existed, ensuring that the uploaded files remain synchronized across these multiple servers then becomes a major operational concern. While there are many solutions to this particular problem (for example, distributed filesystem protocols such as NFS, uploading the assets to remote storage such as Amazon's **Simple Storage Service (S3)**, and so on), they all require additional thought and consideration to evaluate their pros and cons and significant changes to your application's structure.

Testing the photo uploads

As we're on somewhat of a testing roll, let's keep this ball rolling by writing some simple tests in order to validate the behavior of our UploadPhoto resource in tests/test_photos.py. First, let's try to upload some binary data with an unauthenticated request:

```
import io
import base64
from application.models import User, Photo


def test_unauthenticated_form_upload_of_simulated_file(session,
client):
    """Ensure that we can't upload a file via un-authed form POST."""

    data = dict(
        file=(io.BytesIO(b'A test file.'), 'test.png'))

    response = client.post('/photos', data=data)
    assert response.status_code == 401
```

Then, let's check the obvious success path with a properly authenticated request:

```
def test_authenticated_form_upload_of_simulated_file(session, client):
    """Upload photo via POST data with authenticated user."""

    password = 'foobar'
    user = User(username='you', email='you@example.com',
        password=password)

    session.add(user)

    data = dict(
        photo=(io.BytesIO(b'A test file.'), 'test.png'))
```

```python
    creds = base64.b64encode(
        b'{0}:{1}'.format(user.username, password)).decode('utf-8')

    response = client.post('/photos', data=data,
        headers={'Authorization': 'Basic ' + creds})

    assert response.status_code == 201
    assert 'Location' in response.headers

    photos = Photo.query.all()
    assert len(photos) == 1

    assert ('/photos/{}'.format(photos[0].id) in
        response.headers['Location'])
```

Finally, let's ensure that when we submit the (optional) comment, it is persisted to the database:

```python
def test_upload_photo_with_comment(session, client):
    """Adds a photo with a comment."""

    password = 'foobar'
    user = User(username='you', email='you@example.com',
    password=password)

    session.add(user)

    data = dict(
        photo=(io.BytesIO(b'A photo with a comment.'),
        'new_photo.png'),
        comment='What an inspiring photo!')

    creds = base64.b64encode(
        b'{0}:{1}'.format(
            user.username, password)).decode('utf-8')

    response = client.post('/photos', data=data,
        headers={'Authorization': 'Basic ' + creds})

    assert response.status_code == 201
    assert 'Location' in response.headers

    photos = Photo.query.all()
    assert len(photos) == 1

    photo = photos[0]
    assert photo.comment == data['comment']
```

Fetching the user's photos

Other than the ability to upload photos, the meat of the Shutterbug application lies in the ability to fetch a list, in a reverse chronological order, of photos that were uploaded by the authenticated user. For this, we will flesh out the `ListPhoto` resource in `application/resources/photos.py`. As we want the ability to paginate this list of returned photos, we will also create a new instance of `RequestParser` to handle the common page/limit query arguments. Additionally, we will use the marshalling feature of Flask-RESTful to serialize the returned `Photo` objects that are returned from SQLAlchemy so that they can then be converted to JSON and sent over the wire to the requesting client.

 Marshalling is something that web applications (and most other kinds of applications!) do all the time even if you might have never heard of the word. Simply, you take the data in some form of an in-memory representation, such as a Python dictionary or list, and convert it to a format that is more suitable for transmission. In the case of our application, this transformation is to JSON and the transmission occurs over HTTP to the client that made the request.

```
from flask.ext.restful import Resource, reqparse, fields, marshal
photos_parser = reqparse.RequestParser()
photos_parser.add_argument('page', type=int, required=False,
        default=1, location='args')
photos_parser.add_argument('limit', type=int, required=False,
        default=10, location='args')


photo_fields = {
    'path': fields.String,
    'comment': fields.String,
    'created_on': fields.DateTime(dt_format='rfc822'),
}


class ListPhoto(Resource):

    method_decorators = [auth.login_required]

    def get(self):
        """Get reverse chronological list of photos for the
        currently authenticated user."""
```

```
data = photos_parser.parse_args(strict=True)
offset = (data['page'] - 1) * data['limit']
photos = g.current_user.photos.order_by(
    models.Photo.created_on.desc()).limit(
    data['limit']).offset(offset)

return marshal(list(photos), photo_fields), 200
```

Note that in the preceding `ListPhoto.get()` handler, we calculated an offset value based on the page and limit that are provided by the request parameters. The page and limit are independent of the size of our dataset and easy to understand for clients that are consuming the API. SQLAlchemy (and most database APIs, for that matter), only understand offset and limit. The conversion formula is a well-known one and is applicable to any sorted dataset.

Summary

This chapter began somewhat differently than the previous ones. Our objective was to create a JSON-based API instead of a typical web application that produced HTML and consumed submitted HTML form data.

We first took a bit of a sidestep to explain the existence and usefulness of Werkzeug and then created a basic API with a Flask extension called Flask-RESTful. Next, we made sure that our API could be protected by requiring authentication and explained the subtle but fundamental difference between authentication and authorization.

We then looked at how we could implement validation rules for our API in order to ensure that clients could create valid resources (for example, new users, upload photos, and so on). We implemented several functional and integration-level unit tests using the `py.test` framework.

We finished off the chapter by implementing the most important feature, photo uploads. We ensured that this feature functioned as expected with a few more test cases and then implemented the reverse chronological view of the photos necessary for a consumer of the API to display the uploaded images to the user. Along the way, we discussed the concept of Werkzeug middlewares, a powerful but often overlooked way of introspecting and (possibly) modifying a request before Flask has had a chance to process it.

In the next chapter, we will explore the usage and creation of command line tools that will allow us to interface and manage our web applications via CLI.

6
Hublot – Flask CLI Tools

Often when administering a web application, there are tasks that we like to accomplish without having to create an entire administrative web interface; even though this may be accomplished relatively easily with tools such as Flask-Admin. Many developers first turn to a shell scripting language. Bash is near universal on most modern Linux operating systems, favored by system administrators, and is powerful enough to script any administrative task that may be required.

While the venerable Bash script is most definitely always an option, it would be nice to write a Python-based script that could utilize some of the application-specific data handling that we have crafted for our web application. In doing so, we can avoid duplicating a fair amount of energy and effort that was put in the painstaking process of creating, testing, and deploying the data models and domain logic that is the core of any web application. This is where Flask-Script comes in.

 At the time of writing this, Flask has not yet shipped the 1.0 release, which includes an integrated CLI script handling via the `Click` library developed by the author of Flask. As the API of the Flask/Click integration may change significantly between now and the release of Flask 1.0, we've chosen to implement the CLI tools discussed in this chapter via the Flask-Script package, which has been the de facto solution for Flask for quite some time now. The creation of administrative tasks via the Click API can, however, be considered for any new Flask application—the fundamental principles are similar enough even though the implementations differ greatly.

In addition to the infrequent tasks that we may require of a shell script, such as exporting computed data, sending e-mails to a subset of users, and so on, there are certain tasks from our previous applications that may be ported over to the Flask-Script CLI commands:

- Creating/deleting our current database schema, thus replacing our `database.py` from previous projects
- Running our Werkzeug development server, replacing `run.py` from previous projects

Additionally, as Flask-Script is the current de facto solution to write reusable CLI scripts for Flask applications, many other extensions publish CLI commands that can be integrated in your existing application.

In this chapter, we will be creating an application that stores the data pulled from the `Github` API in a local database.

> Git is a **distributed version control system** (**DVCS**) that has become incredibly popular in the last few years and with good reason. It has quickly become the go-to version control system for an incredible amount of open source projects written in a variety of languages.
>
> GitHub, the most well-known hosting platform for Git repositories of open and close source code, is also endowed with a wonderfully complete API that allows for a programmatic access to the data and metadata (comments, pull requests, issues, and so on) that is available, depending on the authenticated credentials provided.

To fetch this data, we will create a simple Flask extension to encapsulate the REST-based API queries in order to fetch the relevant data, and we will then use this extension to create a CLI tool (via Flask-Script) that can be manually run or hooked up to a event-based or time-based scheduler, such as cron.

Before we get into any of this, however, let's set up a very simple application skeleton so that we can begin the Flask-Script integration.

Starting off

We once again reach for our basic Blueprint-based application structure and create a whole new virtual environment and directory for this new venture:

```
$ mkdir -p ~/src/hublot && cd ~/src/hublot
$ mkvirtualenv hublot
$ pip install flask flask-sqlalchemy flask-script
```

The application layout that we'll start off with is very similar to what we used in previous Blueprint-based projects, with the main difference being the manage.py script, which will be the main entry point for our Flask-Script CLI commands. Also note the lack of run.py and a database.py, which we alluded to previously and will explain in more detail shortly:

```
├── application
│   ├── __init__.py
│   └── repositories
│       ├── __init__.py
│       └── models.py
└── manage.py
```

In keeping with our previous work, we continue to use the Application Factory pattern to allow the instantiation of our application to happen at runtime instead of at module import time, as we shall do with the Flask-SQLAlchemy extension that we have become quite familiar with.

Our application/__init__.py file contains the following, which you should recognize quite well:

```python
from flask import Flask
from flask.ext.sqlalchemy import SQLAlchemy

# Initialize the db extension, but without configuring
# it with an application instance.
db = SQLAlchemy()


def create_app(config=None):
    app = Flask(__name__)

    if config is not None:
        app.config.from_object(config)

    # Initialize extensions
    db.init_app(app)

    return app
```

Our `application/settings.py` file contains the very basics that we require for a Flask-SQLAlchemy application:

```
SQLALCHEMY_DATABASE_URI = 'sqlite:///../hublot.db'
```

 We will be using SQLite as our database of choice for this particular project; adjust the URI accordingly in case you decide to use a different database.

For the sake of expediency, we'll introduce simplified `Repository` and `Issue` models that will contain the data we want to collect. These models will exist in `application/repositories/models.py`:

```python
from application import db
from sqlalchemy.schema import UniqueConstraint
import datetime


class Repository(db.Model):
    """Holds the meta-information about a particular
    Github repository."""

    # The unique primary key for the local repository record.
    id = db.Column(db.Integer, primary_key=True)

    # The name of the repository.
    name = db.Column(db.String(length=255), nullable=False)

    # The github org/user that owns the repository.
    owner = db.Column(db.String(length=255), nullable=False)

    # The description (if any) of the repository.
    description = db.Column(db.Text())

    #  The date/time that the record was created on.
    created_on = db.Column(db.DateTime(),
        default=datetime.datetime.utcnow, index=True)

    # The SQLAlchemy relation for the issues contained within this
    # repository.
    issues = db.relationship('Issue')

    __table_args__ = (UniqueConstraint('name', 'owner'), )

    def __repr__(self):
        return u'<Repository {}>'.format(self.name)
```

A `Repository` model instance will contain metadata that pertains to a given Git repository hosted on GitHub with a one-to-many relationship to the `Issue` model, which we will define next. The fields that we have declared in this `Repository` class should be self-explanatory for the most part, the one exception being `__table__args__` dunder.

> A **dunder** is a Python-specific neologism that is used to refer to any variable or method that begins with two underscores: a *double underscore* or *dunder*, for short. There are several built-in dunder methods (for example, `__init__`) and attributes (for example, `__name__`), and any attributes / methods / functions that you declare and prefix with two underscores will fall under this category as well.

This class attribute allows us the ability to specify a table-specific configuration to the underlying SQLAlchemy table that is created. In our case, we will use it to specify a UniqueConstraint key on a compound value, the combination of the name and owner, which would otherwise not be possible via the typical attribute-based field definitions.

Additionally, we defined an issues attribute whose value is a relationship to the `Issue` model; this is the classic one-to-many relationship, and accessing the issues attribute of a repository instance will yield the list of issues that are attached to the repository in question.

> Note that the specified relationship does not include any arguments pertaining to the nature of the query or loading behavior of the related data. We are using the default behavior for this application, which is not a good idea for the repositories that contain a significant amount of issues — a dynamic lazyload approach as was used in a previous chapter may be a better choice in such a situation.

The `Issue` model, which we alluded to in the `Repository` model that we defined, is designed to contain the GitHub issue metadata associated with a Git repository hosted here. As issues only make sense in the context of a repository, we ensure that the `repository_id` foreign key exists for all the issues:

```
class Issue(db.Model):
    """Holds the meta information regarding an issue that
    belongs to a repository."""

    # The autoincremented ID of the issue.
```

```
id = db.Column(db.String(length=40), primary_key=True)
# The repository ID that this issue belongs to.


#
# This relationship will produce a `repository` field
# that will link back to the parent repository.
repository_id = db.Column(db.Integer(),
    db.ForeignKey('repository.id'))

# The title of the issue
title = db.Column(db.String(length=255), nullable=False)

# The issue number
number = db.Column(db.Integer(), nullable=False)

state = db.Column(db.Enum('open', 'closed'), nullable=False)

def __repr__(self):
    """Representation of this issue by number."""
    return '<Issue {}>'.format(self.number)
```

Each instance of an `Issue` model will encapsulate a very limited set of information regarding a GitHub issue that was created, including the issue number, state of the issue (*closed* or *open*), and title that was given to the issue.

At this point in previous chapters, we would have created a `database.py` script to initialize the construction of our SQLAlchemy models in our database. In this chapter, however, we will use Flask-Script to write a small CLI command that will do the same thing but provide us with a more consistent framework to write these little administrative tools and avoid the dozens of independent script files that end up plaguing any nontrivial application over time.

The manage.py file

By convention, the main entry point for Flask-Script is a Python file named `manage.py` that we place sibling to the `application/` package as we described in our project layout in the beginning of this chapter. While Flask-Script contains quite a few options — configurations and customizability — we'll use the simplest of the available invocations to encapsulate the functionality of the `database.py` Python script that we used in previous chapters in order to handle the initialization of our database.

We instantiate a `Manager` instance, which will handle the registration of our various commands. The `Manager` constructor takes a Flask application instance as an argument, but it can also (thankfully!) accept a function or class that implements the callable interface that returns an application instance:

```
from flask.ext.script import Manager
from application import create_app, db

# Create the `manager` object with a
# callable that returns a Flask application object.
manager = Manager(app=create_app)
```

Now that we have a `manager` instance, we use the `command` method of this instance to decorate functions that we would like to turn into CLI commands:

```
@manager.command
def init_db():
    """Initialize SQLAlchemy database models."""

    db.create_all()
```

 Note that, by default, the function name that we wrap with the `command` method will be the identifier used in the CLI invocation.

To get the whole thing running, we call the `run` method of the manager instance when we invoke the `manage.py` file directly:

```
if __name__ == '__main__':
    manager.run()
```

At this point, we can execute our CLI command via the Python interpreter:

```
$ python manage.py init_db
```

Assuming everything worked as expected, we should see no results (or errors, for that matter) and our database should be initialized with the tables, columns, and indexes that we specified in our model definitions.

Let's create a diametrically opposite command that will allow us to destroy our local database; this can sometimes be handy when making a lot of changes to our data model during development:

```
@manager.command
def drop_db():
```

```
if prompt_bool(
    "Are you sure you want to lose all your data"):
    db.drop_all()
```

We invoke this newly created `drop_db` command in exactly the same manner as we invoked the previously defined `init_db` command:

```
$ python manage.py drop_db
```

The built-in default commands

In addition to giving us the ability to quickly define our own CLI commands, Flask-Script includes a few defaults so that we don't have write them ourselves:

```
usage: manage.py [-?] {shell,drop_db,init_db,runserver} ...


positional arguments:
  {shell,drop_db,init_db,runserver}
    shell            Runs a Python shell inside Flask application
                     context.

    drop_db
    init_db          Initialize SQLAlchemy database models.
    runserver        Runs the Flask development server i.e.
                     app.run()


optional arguments:
  -?, --help              show this help message and exit
```

 Flask-Script automatically generates a help text for the registered commands based on docstrings of the relevant functions. Additionally, running the manage.py script without a specified command or with the help option will display the full list of the top-level commands available.

If, for whatever reason, we'd like to customize the defaults, it's relatively easy to accomplish. For example, we need the development server to run on port 6000 instead of the 5000 default:

```
from flask.ext.script import Manager, prompt_bool, Server
# …

if __name__ == '__main__':
```

```
    manager.add_command('runserver', Server(port=6000))
    manager.run()
```

Here, we've used the alternative method of defining a CLI command using the `manager.add_command` method, which takes a name and subclass of `flask.ext.script.command` as the second argument.

Similarly, we can override the default shell command so that our interactive Python shell contains a reference to our configured Flask-SQLAlchemy database object in addition to the Flask app object:

```
def _context():
    """Adds additional objects to our default shell context."""
    return dict(db=db, repositories=repositories)


if __name__ == '__main__':
    manager.add_command('runserver', Server(port=6000))
    manager.add_command('shell', Shell(make_context=_context))
    manager.run()
```

We can verify that our `db` object has been included by executing the `manage.py` script to invoke the interactive shell:

```
$ python manage.py shell
```

```
>>> type(db)
<class 'flask_sqlalchemy.SQLAlchemy'>
>>>
```

Verify that the default Flask application server runs on the port that we specified:

```
$ python manage.py runserver
 * Running on http://127.0.0.1:6000/ (Press CTRL+C to quit)
```

Flask-Script provides several configuration options for the default `runserver` and `shell` commands, including the ability to disable them completely if you want. You can consult the online documentation for additional details.

The Flask-Script commands across Blueprints

The ability to create ad hoc CLI commands in our application-level `manage.py` is both a blessing and curse: A blessing because it requires very little boilerplate to get up and running and a curse because it can very easily spiral into an unmanageable mess of code.

To stave off this somewhat inevitable end state for any nontrivial application, we will use the underutilized feature of submanagers in Flask-Script in order to create a set of CLI commands that will live inside a blueprint but will be accessible via the standard manage.py invocation. This should allow us to keep the domain logic for our command-line interfaces in the same location(s) as the domain logic for our web-based components.

Submanagers

Our first Flask-Script submanager will contain the logic to parse a GitHub project URL to the component pieces that we require to create a valid Repository model record:

```
$ python manage.py repositories add "https://github.com/mitsuhiko/flask"\
    --description="Main Flask repository"
```

The general idea is that we'd like to be able to create a new Repository object with the name, owner, and description parsed from the positional and named arguments provided to the "add" function of the "repositories" submanager.

Let's get started by creating the module that will contain our repository CLI commands in application/repositories/cli.py with an empty add function for the moment:

```
from flask.ext.script import Manager

repository_manager = Manager(
    usage="Repository-based CLI actions.")



@repository_manager.command
def add():
    """Adds a repository to our database."""
    pass
```

Note that our repository_manager instance was created without an application instance or a callable that will return an application instance. Instead of providing the application object here, we will register our newly created submanager instance with our main application manager:

```
from flask.ext.script import Manager, prompt_bool, Server, Shell
from application import create_app, db, repositories
from application.repositories.cli import repository_manager

# Create the `manager` object with a
# callable that returns a Flask application object.
```

```
manager = Manager(app=create_app)

# …
# …

if __name__ == '__main__':
    manager.add_command('runserver', Server(port=6000))
    manager.add_command('shell', Shell(make_context=_context))
    manager.add_command('repositories', repository_manager)
    manager.run()
```

This will let us invoke the `repositories` manager and show us the available subcommands:

```
$ python manage.py repositories --help
usage: Repository-based CLI actions.


Repository-based CLI actions.


positional arguments:
  {add}
    add        Adds a repository to our database.


optional arguments:
  -?, --help  show this help message and exit
```

While this will produce no results (due to the function body being a simple pass statement), we can invoke our `add` subcommand:

```
$ python manage.py repositories add
```

The required and optional arguments

Any command registered with a Flask-Script manager may have zero or many required arguments in addition to any number of optional arguments with arbitrary defaults.

Our `add` command requires one mandatory argument, the URL of the repository to be added to our database, and one optional argument, a description of this repository. The command decorator takes care of a large number of the most basic cases, turning named function arguments to their CLI argument equivalents and function arguments with default values to optional CLI arguments.

This means that we can specify the following function declaration to match what we wrote down previously:

```
@repository_manager.command
def add(url, description=None):
    """Adds a repository to our database."""

    print url, description
```

This allows us to capture the arguments provided to our CLI manager and have them readily available in our function body:

```
$ python manage.py repositories add "https://github.com/mitsuhiko/flask"
--description="A repository to add!"


https://github.com/mitsuhiko/flask A repository to add!
```

As we've managed to properly encode the desired interface for the CLI tool, let's add some parsing to extract out the relevant bits and pieces that we want from the URL:

```
@repository_manager.command
def add(url, description=None):
    """Adds a repository to our database."""

    parsed = urlparse(url)

    # Ensure that our repository is hosted on github
    if parsed.netloc != 'github.com':
        print "Not from Github! Aborting."
        return 1

    try:
        _, owner, repo_name = parsed.path.split('/')
    except ValueError:
        print "Invalid Github project URL format!"
        return 1
```

 We follow the *nix convention of returning a non-zero value between 1 and 127 (the convention is to return 2 for syntax errors and 1 for any other kind of error) when a script encounters an error condition. As we expect our script to successfully add a repository object to our database, any situation where this does not occur could be considered an error condition and should thus return a non-zero value.

Now that we capture and process the CLI arguments correctly, let's use this data to create our `Repository` objects and persist them to our database:

```python
from flask.ext.script import Manager
from urlparse import urlparse
from application.repositories.models import Repository
from application import db
import sqlalchemy

# …

@repository_manager.command
def add(url, description=None):
    """Adds a repository to our database."""

    parsed = urlparse(url)

    # Ensure that our repository is hosted on github
    if parsed.netloc != 'github.com':
        print "Not from Github! Aborting."
        return 1

    try:
        _, owner, repo_name = parsed.path.split('/')
    except ValueError:
        print "Invalid Github project URL format!"
        return 1

    repository = Repository(name=repo_name, owner=owner)
    db.session.add(repository)

    try:
        db.session.commit()
    except sqlalchemy.exc.IntegrityError:
        print "That repository already exists!"
        return 1

    print "Created new Repository with ID: %d" % repository.id
    return 0
```

 Note that we have taken care of the situation where a duplicate repository (that is, with the same name and from the same owner) is added to the database. Without capturing `IntegrityError`, the CLI command would fail and spit out a stack trace indicating the unhandled exception.

Running our newly implemented CLI command now yields the following:

```
$ python manage.py repositories add "https://github.com/mitsuhiko/flask"
--description="A repository to add!"


Created new Repository with ID: 1
```

The successful creation of our `Repository` object may be verified in our database. For SQLite, the following would suffice:

```
$ sqlite3 hublot.db
SQLite version 3.8.5 2014-08-15 22:37:57
Enter ".help" for usage hints.


sqlite> select * from repository;


1|flask|mitsuhiko|A repository to add!|2015-07-22 04:00:36.080829
```

Flask extensions – the basics

We spent a great deal of time installing, configuring, and using various Flask extensions (Flask-Login, Flask-WTF, Flask-Bcrypt, and others). They provide us with a consistent interface to configure third-party libraries and tools and often integrate some Flask-specific niceties that make application development just a bit more enjoyable. One thing that we have not touched upon, however, is how to build your own Flask extension.

 We will only be looking at the framework necessary to create a valid Flask extension to be used locally in a project. If you desire to package your custom extension and publish it on PyPi or GitHub, you will need to implement the proper `setup.py` and setuptools machinery to make this possible. You can follow the setuptools documentation for further details.

When should an extension be used?

A Flask extension usually falls under one of the following two categories:

- Encapsulating the functionality provided by a third-party library, ensuring that this third-party library will function correctly when multiple Flask applications exist in the same process, and possibly adding some convenient functions/objects that make the integration with Flask more concrete; for example, Flask-SQLAlchemy

- The codification of patterns and behaviors that do not require a third-party library but ensure a set of consistent functionalities for an application; for example, Flask-Login

The majority of the Flask extensions that you will encounter in the wild or develop yourself will fall under the first category. The second category is a bit of an outlier and often arises from common patterns observed in multiple applications that are then abstracted and refined to the point where they can be put in an extension.

Our extension – GitHubber

The extension that we will build in this chapter will encapsulate a small portion of the Github API that will allow us to fetch the list of issues for a given repository that we previously tracked.

 The Github API allows for more functionalities than what we need it for and the documentation is excellent. Additionally, there exist several third-party Python libraries that encapsulate much of the Github API, of which we will be using one.

To simplify the interaction with GitHub's v3 API, we're going to install the github3. py Python package to our local virtual environment:

```
$ pip install github3.py
```

As we're developing the extension in our Hublot application, we're not going to introduce the additional complexity of a separate project for the custom Flask extension. If you intend, however, to release and/or distribute an extension, you'll want to ensure that it is structured in such a way that it can be made available via the Python Package Index and installable via setuptools (or distutils, if you'd rather only use packaging tools that are included in the standard library).

Let's create an `extensions.py` module sibling to `application/repositories/` `package` and introduce the basic structure that any Flask extension should contain:

```
class Githubber(object):
    """
    A Flask extension that wraps necessary configuration
    and functionality for interacting with the Github API
    via the `github3.py` 3rd party library.
    """

    def __init__(self, app=None):
        """
        Initialize the extension.

        Any default configurations that do not require
        the application instance should be put here.
        """

        if app:
            self.init_app(app)

    def init_app(self, app):
        """
        Initialize the extension with any application-level
        Configuration requirements.
        """
        self.app = app
```

For most extensions, this is all that is required. Note that the basic extension is a plain old Python object (colloquially referred to as a POPO) definition, augmented with an `init_app` instance method. This method is not strictly necessary. If you don't plan on having the extension use the Flask application object (for example, to load configuration values) or if you have no intention of using the application factory pattern, then `init_app` is superfluous and can be omitted.

We flesh out the extension by adding a few configuration-level checks to ensure that we have `GITHUB_USERNAME` and `GITHUB_PASSWORD` for API-authenticated API access. Additionally, we store the current extension object instance in `app.extensions`, which makes the dynamic usage/loading of the extension more straightforward (among other things):

```
    def init_app(self, app):
        """
        Initialize the extension with any application-level
        Configuration requirements.

        Also store the initialized extension and application state
```

```
to the `app.extensions`
"""

if not hasattr(app, 'extensions'):
    app.extensions = {}

if app.config.get('GITHUB_USERNAME') is None:
    raise ValueError(
        "Cannot use Githubber extension without "
        "specifying the GITHUB_USERNAME.")

if app.config.get('GITHUB_PASSWORD') is None:
    raise ValueError(
        "Cannot use Githubber extension without "
        "specifying the GITHUB_PASSWORD.")

# Store the state of the currently configured extension in
# `app.extensions`.
app.extensions['githubber'] = self
self.app = app
```

Making authenticated requests to the Github API requires some form of authentication. GitHub supports several of these methods but the simplest is specifying the username and password for the account. Generally, this is not something that you want to ask your users to give you: it's better to use the OAuth authorization flow for these situations in order to avoid storing user passwords in cleartext. However, for our rather simple application and custom extension, we'll forgo the extended OAuth implementation (we'll look at OAuth more extensively in a later chapter) and use the username and password combination.

On its own, the extension that we created doesn't do very much. Let's fix this by adding a property-decorated method that instantiates the github3.py Github API client library:

```
from github3 import login


class Githubber(object):
    # ...
    def __init__(self, app=None):

        self._client = None
        # ...
```

```
@property
def client(self):
    if self._client:
        return self._client

    gh_client = login(self.app.config['GITHUB_USERNAME'],
            password=self.app.config['GITHUB_PASSWORD'])

    self._client = gh_client
    return self._client
```

In the preceding `client` method, we've implemented the caching property pattern, which will ensure that we only ever instantiate a single `github3.py` client per created application instance. Additionally, the extension will load the `Github` API client lazily on the first access, which is generally a good idea. This lets us use the client property of the extension to interface directly with the `github3.py` Python library once the application object has been initialized.

Now that we have the basic setup for our custom Flask extension, let's initialize it and configure the extension itself in our application factory in `application/__init__.py`:

```
from flask import Flask
from flask.ext.sqlalchemy import SQLAlchemy
from application.extensions import Githubber

# …
hubber = Githubber()

def create_app(config=None):
    app = Flask(__name__)
    # …

    # Initialize any extensions and bind blueprints to the
    # application instance here.
    db.init_app(app)
    hubber.init_app(app)

    return app
```

Note the `hubber = Githubber()` initialization and assignment that happens outside of the factory itself, but the actual `init_app(app)` method call and implied extension configuration that occurs in the factory after we've initialized a Flask application object. You've probably noticed this split pattern (and we've discussed it several times in previous chapters as well), but now you've seen the reasoning behind it via the development of your own extension.

With this in mind, we add an additional function to our `application/repositories/cli.py` module for some additional CLI tooling power:

```
from flask.ext.script import Manager
from urlparse import urlparse
from application.repositories.models import Repository, Issue
from application import db, hubber
import sqlalchemy

# …

@repository_manager.command
def fetch_issues(repository_id):
    """Fetch all commits for the given Repository."""

    try:
        repo = Repository.query.get(repository_id)
    except sqlalchemy.orm.exc.NoResultFound:
        print "No such repository ID!"
        return 1

    r = hubber.client.repository(repo.owner, repo.name)
    issues = []

    for issue in r.iter_issues():
        i = Issue(repository_id=repo.id, title=issue.title,
                number=issue.number, state=issue.state)

        issues.append(i)

    db.session.add_all(issues)

    print "Added {} issues!".format(len(issues))
```

After fetching the repository object from the database (based on the ID value specified via the CLI argument), we invoke the `client.repository()` method of our `Githubber` extension, which we imported as `hubber`, the name it was assigned during the instantiation in the factory preamble. As a part of our extension takes care of initializing it with the credentials required to make authenticated requests, we don't need to handle this in the CLI tool that invokes it.

Once we've obtained a reference to the remote GitHub repository, we iterate over the registered issues via the `iter_issues()` method provided by `github3.py` and then create the `Issue` instances that we persist to the SQLAlchemy session.

> A welcome improvement to the current `Issue` model would be the introduction of a compound index on `repository_id` and the number with a unique constraint to ensure that imported issues are not duplicated in case we run the preceding command more than once on the same repository.
>
> Handling of the raised exception on the insertion of a duplicate would then need to happen in the preceding CLI command as well. The implementation is left as a (relatively simple) exercise for the reader.

These types of CLI tools are very useful to script actions and behaviors that could be considered too costly to occur in-band of a current user request of a typical web application. The last thing that you want is for a user of your application to wait seconds, if not minutes, for some action to complete that you have almost no control over. Instead, it's better to have these events occur out of band. Popular methods of accomplishing this include cron jobs and job/task queues such as those implemented by Celery (which may be event-driven instead of scheduled to run at fixed time intervals such as cron jobs), to name a few.

Summary

After reading through this chapter, you should be more familiar with the inner workings of Flask extensions and command line-based interfaces to the application via Flask-Script.

We began by creating a simple application for the data corresponding to the repositories and issues hosted on GitHub and then installed and configured our `manage.py` script to act as our bridge for the Flask-Script default CLI runserver and shell commands. We added the `drop_db` and `init_db` global commands to replace the `database.py` script that we used in previous chapters. Once this was in place, we turned our attention to creating the script submanagers in Blueprints that we could control via the main `manage.py` interface script.

Finally, we implemented our own Flask extension that wrapped some basic configuration and resource instantiation of the `github3.py` `Github` API client. Once this was finished, we went back to our previously created submanager script and added the required functionality to fetch the list of issues stored on GitHub for a given repository ID.

In the next chapter, we will take a deeper dive into third-party APIs, where we will build an application that uses the OAuth authorization protocol in order to implement user account creation and login via Twitter and Facebook.

7
Dinnerly – Recipe Sharing

In this chapter, we will explore modern methods of the so-called social login, where we allow a user to authenticate with our application using derived credentials from another web application. Currently, the most widespread third-party applications that support this mechanism are, somewhat unsurprisingly, Twitter and Facebook.

While there exist several other widespread web applications that support this type of integration (for example, LinkedIn, Dropbox, Foursquare, Google, and GitHub to name a few), the majority of your potential users will be in possession of at least one account on either Twitter or Facebook, the two major social networks of this time.

To do this, we will be adding, configuring, and deploying the Flask-OAuthlib extension. This extension abstracts out some of the usual difficulties and roadblocks that are often experienced when dealing with an OAuth-based authorization flow (which we will explain shortly) and includes functionalities to quickly set up the defaults required to negotiate the provider / consumer / resource owner token exchange. As a bonus, the extension will provide us with the ability to interact with the authenticated APIs of these remote services on behalf of the user.

First OAuth

Let's get this out of the way: OAuth can be somewhat difficult to grasp. Adding to this fire is the fact that the OAuth framework/protocol has gone through a major revision in the last few years. Version 2 was published in 2012, but due to a variety of factors, there are some web applications that continue to implement the OAuth v1 protocol.

> OAuth 2.0 is not backwards compatible with OAuth 1.0. Moreover, OAuth 2.0 is less of a formal protocol specification and more of an authorization framework specification. Most OAuth 2.0 implementations across modern web applications are not interoperable.

For the sake of simplicity, we'll view a high-level overview of the general terms, vocabulary, and functionalities of the OAuth 2.0 authorization framework. Version 2 is the simpler of the two specifications and with good reason: one of the design goals of the latter was to make client implementations simpler and less prone to error. Much of the terminology is similar, if not identical, across the two versions.

While the intricacies of the OAuth authorization exchanges will mostly be abstracted away from us thanks to the Flask-OAuthlib extension and underlying Python packages that handle the real grunt work, a cursory level of knowledge regarding the OAuth authorization framework (specifically the most common authorization grant flows) for web applications and the typical implementations will be beneficial.

Why use OAuth?

One of the great sins of proper online personal security is the reuse of access credentials across different services. This opens you up to a variety of security-related issues if the credentials you use for one application are compromised. You now have the possibility of being compromised on all the applications where this same set of credentials are used and the only way to fix this post facto would be to go and change your credentials everywhere.

Even worse than reusing the credentials across the different services is having a user willingly turn over their credentials for a third-party service, say Twitter, to some other service, say Foursquare, so that the latter can make requests to Twitter on behalf of the user (for example, posting check-ins to their Twitter timeline). While not immediately obvious, one of the problems with this approach is that the credentials must be stored in plain text.

This situation is not ideal for a variety of reasons, and some of these reasons are not things that you, as an application developer, can control.

OAuth, in both version 1 and version 2 of the framework, attempt to solve the problem of cross-application shared credentials by creating an open standard for API access delegation. The principle goal of OAuth's original design was to ensure that a user of application A could delegate access to application B on their behalf and also ensure that application B was never in possession of the credentials that could compromise the user account on application A.

While an application in possession of delegated credentials can abuse these credentials to perform some unsavory actions, the root credentials have never been shared and thus the owner of the account can simply invalidate the delegated credentials that have been abused. If the root account credentials had simply been given to the third-party application, then this latter could have taken complete control of the account by changing all of the primary authentication information (username, e-mail, password, and so on), which would effectively hijack the account.

Terminology

Most of the confusion about OAuth usage and implementation stems from a misunderstanding of the essential vocabulary and terminology that is used to describe the basic authorization flow. Even worse, there are several popular web applications that have implemented OAuth (in some form or another) and decided to use their own vocabulary for portions of the protocol/framework instead of those that have been decided upon in the official RFC.

An RFC, or a Request For Comments, is a memorandum-style publication of a document or set of documents from the **Internet Engineering Task Force (IETF)**, which is the principal body that governs the open standards on which most of the Internet is built upon. RFCs are usually denoted by a numeric code, which uniquely identifies them in the IETF. For example, the OAuth 2.0 authorization framework RFC is number 6749 and can be found in its entirety on the IETF website.

To help alleviate some of this confusion, here's a simplified description of what most of the essential components of an OAuth implementation mean in plain English:

- **Consumer**: This is the application that is making the request on behalf of the user. In our particular case, the Dinnerly application is considered the consumer. Confusingly enough, the official OAuth specification refers to the client instead of the consumer. Even more confusingly, some applications use the consumer *and* client terms. Usually, a consumer is represented by a key and secret that must be kept in your application configuration, and they must be well-guarded. If a malicious entity were to gain access to your consumer key and secret, they could then pretend to be your application when making authorized requests with the third-party provider.

- **Provider**: This is the third-party service that the consumer is attempting to access on behalf of a user. In our case, Twitter and Facebook are the providers that we will be using for our application signing in. Other examples of providers could be GitHub, LinkedIn, Google, and any other service that offers a grant-based OAuth authorization flow.

- **Resource owner**: This is the entity that is capable of consenting to the delegated resource access. In most cases, the resource owner is an end user of both the applications (for example, Twitter and Dinnerly) in question.

- **Access token(s)**: This is a credential that the client uses to make requests to the provider on behalf of a user in order to access the protected resources. The token can be linked with a particular permission scope, which limits what resources it can access. Additionally, the access token may expire after a certain amount of time determined by the provider; at which point the use of a refresh token is required to obtain a new, valid access token.

- **Authorization server**: This is the server (usually represented by a URI endpoint) that is responsible for issuing access tokens to the consumer application after the resource owner has consented to delegating their access.

- **Flow type**: The OAuth 2.0 framework provides outlines of several different flows for authorization. Some are best suited for command-line applications where no web browser is present, others are better suited for native mobile applications, and some have also been created to connect devices that have very limited access capabilities (for example, if you want to delegate your Twitter account privileges to your Internet-enabled toaster). The authorization flow that we are most interested in, unsurprisingly, is the one designed for basic web browser-based access.

With the preceding list of vocabulary, you should now be able to comprehend the official abstract protocol flow that is listed in the official OAuth 2.0 RFC:

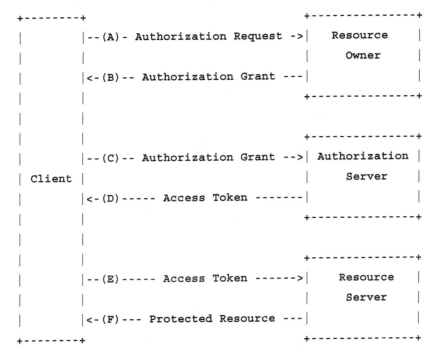

The following description of the steps listed in the flow diagram has been taken from RFC 6749 and made a bit more relevant for our purposes:

1. The client (or consumer) requests the resource owner to grant an authorization. This is usually where the user is redirected to a login screen on the remote provider, say Twitter, where it is explained that the client application wishes to access the protected resources that you control. On agreeing to this, we enter the next step.

2. The client receives an authorization grant from the resource owner (user), which is a temporary credential representing the resource owner's authorization for the particular type of authorization flow that the provider has implemented. This is typically an authorization code grant flow for most web applications.

3. Once the client has received the grant credentials, it sends them to the authorization server to request an authentication token on behalf of the resource owner.

4. The authorization server validates the grant credentials and authenticates the client making the request. Upon fulfilling these two requirements, the server returns a valid authentication token to the client that can then be used to make authenticated requests to the provider on behalf of the user.

So what's wrong with OAuth 1.0?

In theory: not much. In practice: it's somewhat difficult and extremely error prone to be implemented correctly for the consumer.

The primary difficulties in implementing and using an OAuth 1.0 provider revolve around consumer applications not performing the required cryptographic request signing properly. The arguments and parameters had to be collected from the query string in addition to the request body and various OAuth parameters (for example, oauth_nonce, oauth_signature_method, oauth_timestamp, and so on) and then URL-encoded (meaning that non-URL safe values are specially encoded to ensure they are transmitted correctly). Once the key/value pairs have been encoded, they must then be sorted lexicographically by key (remember, the encoded key and not the raw key value) and then concatenated to a single string using typical URL parameter separators. Additionally, the HTTP verb that is to be used to submit the request (for example, GET or POST) must be prepended to the string that we just created and then followed by the URL that the request will be sent to. Finally, the signing key is to be constructed from the consumer secret key and an OAuth token secret and then passed to an implementation of the HMAC-SHA1 hashing algorithm along with the payload that we constructed earlier.

Assuming that you got all this correct (and it's incredibly easy to make a simple mistake such as sorting your keys alphabetically instead of lexicographically), only then would the request be considered valid. Moreover, in the event of a miscalculated signature, there's no simple way to determine where the mistake was made.

One of the reasons that this rather complex process is required for OAuth 1.0 is that a design goal of this protocol was that it should function across insecure protocols such as HTTP, but still ensure that the request has not been modified by a malicious party along the way.

OAuth 2.0, while not universally accepted as a worthy successor to OAuth 1.0, has greatly simplified the implementation by simply requiring that all the communication occur over HTTPS.

Three-legged authorization

In the so-called three-legged authorization flow for the OAuth framework, an application (consumer) makes requests on behalf of a user (resource owner) in order to access the resources present on a remote service (provider).

There also exists a two-legged authorization flow, which is primarily used for application-to-application access where a resource owner is not required to consent to delegated access to the protected resources. Twitter, for example, implements both two-legged and three-legged authorization flows, but the former does not have the same access scope as the latter in terms of resource access and imposed API rate limits.

This is what Flask-Social will allow us to implement for Twitter and Facebook, the two providers that we have chosen, where our application will act as the consumer. The end result will be that our Dinnerly application will be in possession of access tokens for both the providers that will allow us to make authenticated API requests on behalf of our users (the resource owners), which is necessary to implement any sort of cross-social network posting functionality.

Setting up the application

Once again, let's set up a barebones folder for our project along with the associated virtual environment in order to isolate our application dependencies:

```
$ mkdir -p ~/src/dinnerly
$ mkvirtualenv dinnerly
$ cd ~/src/dinnerly
```

Once created, let's install the basic packages that we will require including Flask itself along with the Flask-OAuthlib extension, our trusty friend Flask-SQLAlchemy, and Flask-Login, which we used in a previous chapter:

```
$ pip install flask flask-oauthlib flask-sqlalchemy flask-login flask-wtf
```

We'll utilize our trusty Blueprint-based application structure that has served us so well in the past chapters to ensure a solid foundation. For now, we'll have a single users Blueprint where the OAuth handling will be taken care of:

```
-run.py
-application
├── __init__.py
└── users
    ├── __init__.py
    ├── models.py
    └── views.py
```

Once the very basic folder and file structure has been established, let's use an application factory to create our main application object. For now, all we're going to do is instantiate a very simple application with a Flask-SQLAlchemy database connection in `application/__init__.py`:

```
from flask import Flask
from flask.ext.sqlalchemy import SQLAlchemy

# Deferred initialization of the db extension
db = SQLAlchemy()


def create_app(config=None):
    app = Flask(__name__, static_folder=None)

    if config is not None:
        app.config.from_object(config)

    db.init_app(app)
    return app
```

To ensure that we can actually run the application and create the database, let's use the simple `run.py` and `database.py` scripts that we will place sibling to the `application` folder. The contents of `run.py` are similar to what we used in the previous chapters:

```
from application import create_app

app = create_app(config='settings')
app.run(debug=True)
```

 Later on in this chapter, we will explore alternative methods of running the Dinnerly application, most of which are more well-suited to production deployments. The Werkzeug development server that is invoked on `app.run()` is highly unsuitable for anything other than local development.

Our `database.py` is, quite similarly, simple and to the point:

```
from application import db, create_app
app = create_app(config='settings')
db.app = app

db.create_all()
```

This will allow us to create the relevant schema in our database based on our model definitions, which have not yet been declared; running the script right now will essentially be a no op. This is okay! We have much to do before this becomes useful.

Declaring our models

As is the case with most applications, we begin by declaring our data models and any relationships that they require. We will, of course, require a `User` model, which will be the centerpiece of the OAuth authorization and token exchange.

As you may recall from our brief overview of the OAuth terminology and the basic three-legged authorization grant flow, the access tokens are what allow a client (our Dinnerly application) to query resources on a remote service provider (for example, Twitter or Facebook). As we need these tokens to make requests to the listed service providers, we're going to want to store them somewhere so that we can use them without having the user reauthenticate for every action; this would be quite tedious.

Our `User` model will be quite similar to the `User` models that we have used previously (although we removed a few attributes to simplify things a bit), and we'll place it in the obvious location of `application/users/models.py`:

```
import datetime
from application import db

class User(db.Model):

    # The primary key for each user record.
    id = db.Column(db.Integer, primary_key=True)

    # The username for a user. Might not be
    username = db.Column(db.String(40))

    #  The date/time that the user account was created on.
    created_on = db.Column(db.DateTime,
        default=datetime.datetime.utcnow)

    def __repr__(self):
        return '<User {!r}>'.format(self.username)
```

 Note that we have not included anything regarding a password. As the intent of this application is to require either Facebook or Twitter to create an account and log in, we've eschewed the typical username/password credentials combination in favor of delegating authentication to one of these third-party services.

To help with our user session management, we're going to reuse the Flask-Login extension that we explored in a previous chapter. In case you've forgotten, one of the basic requirements of the extension is to have four methods declared on whatever model you are using to represent an authenticated user: `is_authenticated`, `is_active`, `is_anonymous`, and `get_id`. Let's append the most basic versions of these methods to our already declared `User` model:

```python
class User(db.Model):

    # ...

    def is_authenticated(self):
        """All our registered users are authenticated."""
        return True

    def is_active(self):
        """All our users are active."""
        return True

    def is_anonymous(self):
        """All users are not in an anonymous state."""
        return False

    def get_id(self):
        """Get the user ID as a Unicode string."""
        return unicode(self.id)
```

Now, you may have noticed that there are no declared attributes on the `User` model for our Twitter or Facebook access tokens. Adding these attributes are an option, of course, but we're going to use a slightly different approach that requires more up-front complexity and will allow more providers to be added without polluting our `User` model more than necessary.

Our approach will center on the idea of creating multiple one-to-one data relationships between a user and the various provider types that will be represented by their own models. Let's add our first provider model in `application/users/models.py` to the store:

```python
class TwitterConnection(db.Model):

    # The primary key for each connection record.
    id = db.Column(db.Integer, primary_key=True)

    # Our relationship to the User that this
    # connection belongs to.
```

```
user_id = db.Column(db.Integer(),
    db.ForeignKey('user.id'), nullable=False, unique=True)

# The twitter screen name of the connected account.
screen_name = db.Column(db.String(), nullable=False)

# The Twitter ID of the connected account
twitter_user_id = db.Column(db.Integer(), nullable=False)

# The OAuth token
oauth_token = db.Column(db.String(), nullable=False)

# The OAuth token secret
oauth_token_secret = db.Column(db.String(), nullable=False)
```

The preceding model declares a foreign key relationship to the `User` model via the `user_id` attribute, and the additional fields (other than the primary key) store the requisite OAuth token and secret to make authenticated requests to the Twitter API on behalf of the user. Additionally, we store the Twitter `screen_name` and `twitter_user_id` to give us the option of using this value as username for the related user. Keeping the Twitter user ID around helps us match users on Twitter with local Dinnerly users (as `screen_name` can be changed but the IDs are immutable).

Once the `TwitterConnection` model is defined, let's add the relationship to the `User` model so that we can access the associated credentials via the `twitter` attribute:

```
Class User(db.Model):
  # ...

  twitter = db.relationship("TwitterConnection", uselist=False,
    backref="user")
```

This establishes a very simple one-to-one relationship between `User` and `TwitterConnection`. The `uselist=False` argument ensures that the configured attribute will refer to a scalar value instead of a list, which would be the default for a one-to-many relationship.

Accordingly, once we've obtained a user object instance, we can access the associated `TwitterConnection` model data via `user.twitter`. If no credentials have been attached, then this will return `None`; if there are attached credentials, we can access the subattributes just as you expect: `user.twitter.oauth_token`, `user.twitter.screen_name`, and others.

Let's do the same for the equivalent `FacebookConnection` model, which has similar attributes. The difference from the `TwitterConnection` model is that Facebook OAuth only requires a single token (instead of a combination token and secret), and we can choose to store the Facebook-specific ID and name (whereas in the other model, we stored the Twitter `screen_name`):

```python
class FacebookConnection(db.Model):

    # The primary key for each connection record.
    id = db.Column(db.Integer, primary_key=True)

    # Our relationship to the User that this
    # connection belongs to.
    user_id = db.Column(db.Integer(),
        db.ForeignKey('user.id'), nullable=False)

    # The numeric Facebook ID of the user that this
    # connection belongs to.
    facebook_id = db.Column(db.Integer(), nullable=False)

    # The OAuth token
    access_token = db.Column(db.String(), nullable=False)

    # The name of the user on Facebook that this
    # connection belongs to.
    name = db.Column(db.String())
```

Once we've established this model, we'll want to introduce the relationship to our `User` model as we did for the `TwitterConnection` model previously:

```python
class User(db.Model):

    # ...

    facebook = db.relationship("FacebookConnection",
        uselist=False, backref="user")
```

The functionality and usage of the preceding `facebook` attribute of a `user` instance is identical to that of the `twitter` attribute that we defined previously.

Handling OAuth in our views

With our basic user and OAuth connection models established, let's start constructing the required Flask-OAuthlib objects to handle the authorization grant flows. The first step is to initialize the extension in the usual way for our application factory. While we're at it, let's also initialize the Flask-Login extension, which we will use to manage authenticated sessions for our logged-in users:

```python
from flask import Flask
from flask.ext.sqlalchemy import SQLAlchemy
from flask_oauthlib.client import OAuth
    from flask.ext.login import LoginManager


# Deferred initialization of our extensions
db = SQLAlchemy()
oauth = OAuth()
login_manager = LoginManager()


def create_app(config=None):
    app = Flask(__name__, static_folder=None)

    if config is not None:
        app.config.from_object(config)

    db.init_app(app)
    oauth.init_app(app)
    login_manager.init_app(app)

    return app
```

Now that we have an `oauth` object available to us, we can instantiate separate OAuth remote application clients for each service provider. Let's place these in our `application/users/views.py` module:

```python
from flask.ext.login import login_user, current_user
from application import oauth

twitter = oauth.remote_app(
    'twitter',
    consumer_key='<consumer key>',
    consumer_secret='<consumer secret>',
    base_url='https://api.twitter.com/1.1/',
    request_token_url='https://api.twitter.com/oauth/request_token',
```

```
    access_token_url='https://api.twitter.com/oauth/access_token',
    authorize_url='https://api.twitter.com/oauth/authenticate')

facebook = oauth.remote_app(
    'facebook',
    consumer_key='<facebook app id>',
    consumer_secret='<facebook app secret>',
    request_token_params={'scope': 'email,publish_actions'},
    base_url='https://graph.facebook.com',
    request_token_url=None,
    access_token_url='/oauth/access_token',
    access_token_method='GET',
    authorize_url='https://www.facebook.com/dialog/oauth')
```

Now, there seems to be quite a lot going on during the instantiation of these OAuth objects, but most of it is simply telling the generic OAuth connection library where the service provider URI endpoints exist for various portions of the three-legged OAuth authorization grant flow. There are, however, a few argument values that you'll need to fill in yourself: the consumer keys (for Twitter) and the application keys (for Facebook). To obtain these, you must register a new OAuth client application on the respective services, and you can do so here:

- Twitter: `https://apps.twitter.com/app/new`, and then navigate to the **Keys and Access Tokens** tab to obtain the consumer key and consumer secret.

- Facebook: `https://developers.facebook.com/apps/` and agree to the terms of service and register your account for application development. Once there, select the website type of application to add and follow the instructions to generate the required application ID and application secret.

In the case of Facebook, we requested the ability to publish to the wall of the user in question via the `publish_actions` value of the scope key in the `request_token_params` argument of the `remote_app` method of the OAuth object that we've created. This is enough for our purposes, but if you want to interact with the Facebook API more than simply pushing status updates, you'll need to request the correct set of permissions. The Facebook documentation has additional information and guidelines on how third-party application developers should use the permission scope values to perform different actions.

Once you've obtained the requisite keys and secrets, insert them where we left placeholders in the preceding `oauth` remote application client configurations.

Now, we need to have our application handle the various portions of the authorization flow that require users to request a grant token from the service provider. We also need our application to handle the callback routes that the service provider will redirect to with the various OAuth tokens and secrets once the process is completed so that we can persist these values to our database.

Let's whip up a users Blueprint to namespace the various routes in `application/users/views.py`, and while we're at it, import a few utilities from Flask and Flask-Login to help our integration:

```
from flask import Blueprint, redirect, url_for, request
from flask.ext.login import login_user, current_user

from application.users.models import (
    User, TwitterConnection, FacebookConnection)
from application import oauth, db, login_manager
import sqlalchemy

users = Blueprint('users', __name__, template_folder='templates')
```

As per the requirements of Flask-Login, we need to define a user_loader function that will fetch a user from our database by the ID:

```
@login_manager.user_loader
def load_user(user_id):
    return User.query.get(int(user_id))
```

In a very similar fashion, Flask-OAuthlib requires us to define a method (per service, of course) that will act as a token getter; while Flask-Login needs user_loader to fetch users from our database by the ID. The OAuthlib needs to have a function that fetches the OAuth token(s) of the currently logged-in user. If no user is currently logged in, then the method should return None, indicating that we should probably start an authorization grant flow to obtain the required tokens:

```
@twitter.tokengetter
def get_twitter_token():
    """Fetch Twitter token from currently logged
    in user."""
    if (current_user.is_authenticated() and
            current_user.twitter):
        return (current_user.twitter.oauth_token,
                current_user.twitter.oauth_token_secret)
    return None

@facebook.tokengetter
def get_facebook_token():
```

```
"""Fetch Facebook token from currently logged
in user."""
if (current_user.is_authenticated() and
        current_user.facebook):
    return (current_user.facebook.oauth_token, )
return None
```

> Note that we used the `current_user` proxy object that
> Flask-Login provides us with in order to access the object
> of the currently authenticated user, and then we call the
> `is_authenticated` method that we defined in our `User`
> model earlier in the chapter.

Following this, we need to define the routes and handlers to kick off the three-legged authorization grant. Our first users Blueprint route will handle attempted logins using Twitter as the third-party provider:

```
@users.route('/login/twitter')
def login_twitter():
    """Kick-off the Twitter authorization flow if
    not currently authenticated."""

    if current_user.is_authenticated():
        return redirect(url_for('recipes.index'))
    return twitter.authorize(
        callback=url_for('.twitter_authorized',
            _external=True))
```

The preceding route first determines if the current user is already authenticated and redirects them to the main `recipes.index` route handler if they are.

> We've set up some redirects for the `recipes.index` route, which
> we have yet to define. If you intend on testing out this part of the
> application before we set these up, you'll have to either add a stub
> page to that Blueprint route or change it to something else.

If the user is not already authenticated, we initiate the authorization grant via the `twitter.authorize` method invocation. This will initiate the OAuth flow, and upon successful completion of the grant (assuming that the user consents to allow our application to access to their third-party protected resources), Twitter will invoke a GET request to the callback URL that we provided as the first argument. This request will contain the OAuth tokens and any additional information that they have deemed useful (such as `screen_name`) in the query arguments, and it's then up to us to handle the request as we would any other and extract out the information that we require.

To this end, we define a `twitter_authorized` route handler whose sole purpose is to extract out OAuth tokens and secrets so that we can persist them in our database and then use the `login_user` function from Flask-Login to create an authenticated user session for our Dinnerly application:

```
@users.route('/login/twitter-authorized')
def twitter_authorized():
  resp = twitter.authorized_response()

  try:
    user = db.session.query(User).join(
      TwitterConnection).filter(
        TwitterConnection.oauth_token ==
          resp['oauth_token']).one()
    except sqlalchemy.orm.exc.NoResultFound:
      credential = TwitterConnection(
        twitter_user_id=int(resp['user_id']),
        screen_name=resp['screen_name'],
        oauth_token=resp['oauth_token'],
        oauth_token_secret=resp['oauth_token_secret'])

      user = User(username=resp['screen_name'])
      user.twitter = credential

      db.session.add(user)
      db.session.commit()
      db.session.refresh(user)

  login_user(user)
  return redirect(url_for('recipes.index'))
```

In the preceding route handler, we first attempt to extract the OAuth data from the grant flow, which is made available to us in `twitter.authorized_response()`.

> If the user decided to decline the authorization grant request, then `twitter.authorized_response()` will return None. Handling this error scenario is left as an exercise for the reader.
>
> Hint: A Flash message and redirect to a page describing what happened are probably a good start!

Once the OAuth tokens have been extracted from the OAuth data response of the grant flow, we check the database to see if a user with this token already exists. If this is the case, then the user has already created an account on Dinnerly and simply wishes to reauthenticate. (Perhaps as they are using a different browser, thus they do not have the previously generated session cookie available.)

If no user in our system has the OAuth token assigned to them, then we create a new User record with the data that we've just received. Once this is persisted to the SQLAlchemy session, we log them in using the login_user function from Flask-Login.

While we focused on the route handlers and Twitter OAuth authorization grant flow here, the process for Facebook is very similar. Our users Blueprint gets two more routes attached, which will handle the logins that want to use Facebook as the third-party service provider:

```python
@users.route('/login/facebook')
def login_facebook():
    """Kick-off the Facebook authorization flow if
    not currently authenticated."""

    if current_user.is_authenticated():
        return redirect(url_for('recipes.index'))
    return facebook.authorize(
        callback=url_for('.facebook_authorized',
            _external=True))
```

We then define the facebook_authorized handler, which will receive the OAuth token parameters via the query arguments, in a very similar manner to the twitter_authorized route handler:

```python
@users.route('/login/facebook-authorized')
def facebook_authorized():
    """Handle the authorization grant & save the token."""

    resp = facebook.authorized_response()
    me = facebook.get('/me')

    try:
        user = db.session.query(User).join(
            FacebookConnection).filter(
                TwitterConnection.oauth_token ==
                    resp['access_token']).one()
    except sqlalchemy.orm.exc.NoResultFound:
        credential = FacebookConnection(
            name=me.data['name'],
```

```
            facebook_id=me.data['id'],
            access_token=resp['access_token'])

        user = User(username=resp['screen_name'])
        user.twitter = credential

        db.session.add(user)
        db.session.commit()
        db.session.refresh(user)

    login_user(user)
    return redirect(url_for('recipes.index'))
```

One nontrivial difference between this handler and the one that we previously defined for Twitter is the invocation of the `facebook.get('/me')` method. Once we've performed the authorization grant exchange, the facebook OAuth object is able to make authenticated requests to the Facebook API on behalf of the user. We will use this newfound ability to query for some basic details regarding the user who delegated the authorization credentials, such as the Facebook ID and name of the user in question. Once obtained, we store this information along with the OAuth credentials for the newly created user.

Creating recipes

Now that we've allowed users to create authenticated accounts on Dinnerly with Twitter or Facebook, we need to create something worth sharing on these social networks! We'll keep things very simple with a `Recipe` model, which we'll create in the `application/recipes/models.py` module:

```python
import datetime
from application import db


class Recipe(db.Model):

    # The unique primary key for each recipe created.
    id = db.Column(db.Integer, primary_key=True)

    # The title of the recipe.
    title = db.Column(db.String())

    # The ingredients for the recipe.
    # For the sake of simplicity, we'll assume ingredients
    # are in a comma-separated string.
```

```
ingredients = db.Column(db.Text())

# The instructions for each recipe.
instructions = db.Column(db.Text())

#   The date/time that the post was created on.
created_on = db.Column(db.DateTime(),
    default=datetime.datetime.utcnow,
    index=True)

# The user ID that created this recipe.
user_id = db.Column(db.Integer(), db.ForeignKey('user.id'))

# User-Recipe is a one-to-many relationship.
user = db.relationship('User',
        backref=db.backref('recipes'))
```

There's nothing incredibly special about the `Recipe` model that we've just defined; it has a title, ingredients, and instructions. Each recipe is owned by a single user, and we've created the requisite relationship-based field and our `ForeignKey` entry in the model so that our data is properly linked together in the usual relational database way. There are a few fields to store the typical things that you'd expect in any recipe: `title`, `ingredients`, and `instructions`. As the point of Dinnerly is to share snippets of recipes on various social networks, we should add a method that will help generate a short summary of a recipe and limit it to fewer than 140 characters (to appease the Twitter API):

```
def summarize(self, character_count=136):
    """
    Generate a summary for posting to social media.
    """

    if len(self.title) <= character_count:
        return self.title

    short = self.title[:character_count].rsplit(' ', 1)[0]
    return short + '...'
```

The preceding `summarize` method will return the title of `Recipe` if the title contains fewer than 140 characters. If it contains more than 140 characters, we will split the string into a list using a space as the delimiter, use `rsplit` (which starts at the end of the string instead of the beginning as `str.split` does), and then append the ellipsis.

The `summarize` method that we just defined will only reliably work for ASCII text. There exist Unicode characters that may resemble a space as represented in the ASCII character set, but our method will not split on these correctly as it's expecting a different character.

Posting recipes to Twitter and Facebook

Upon posting a new recipe, we'd like to automatically post the summary to the services that have been connected for the user in question. There are, of course, many ways to go about this:

- In our yet-to-be defined recipe view handlers, we could call the respective OAuth connection object methods after the successful creation/committing of a `Recipe` object instance

- The user could be required to visit a particular URI (or submit a form with particular data), which would trigger the cross-posting

- When the `Recipe` object is committed to the database, we could listen for the `after_insert` event emitted by SQLAlchemy and push out our summary to the connected social networks then

As the first two options are relatively simple, somewhat boring, and we haven't explored SQLAlchemy events at all in this book so far, the third option is the one that we'll implement.

SQLAlchemy events

One of the less well-known features of SQLAlchemy is the event API, which publishes several core and ORM-level hooks that will allow us to attach to and execute arbitrary code.

The event system is very similar in spirit (if not in implementation) to the Blinker dispatching system that we saw in a previous chapter. Instead of creating, publishing, and consuming blinker-based signals, we are simply going to listen for events published by the SQLAlchemy subsystem.

Most applications will never need to implement handlers for the various events that are published. They are usually the purview of plugins and extensions to SQLAlchemy, which allow the developer to augment the functionality of their application without requiring them to write large amounts of boilerplate connector / adapter / interface logic to interact with these plugins or extensions.

The SQLAlchemy events that we are interested in are categorized under ORM Events. Even in this restricted umbrella of events (there are a plethora of additional published core events that we won't even discuss here), there are still quite a few events. What most developers are interested in, generally, are the mapper-level events:

- `before_insert`: This receives an object instance before an INSERT statement is emitted corresponding to that instance

- `after_insert`: This receives an object instance after an INSERT statement is emitted corresponding to that instance

- `before_update`: This receives an object instance before an UPDATE statement is emitted corresponding to that instance

- `after_update`: This receives an object instance after an UPDATE statement is emitted corresponding to that instance

- `before_delete`: This receives an object instance before a DELETE statement is emitted corresponding to that instance

- `after_delete`: This receives an object instance after a DELETE statement has been emitted corresponding to that instance

Each named event is emitted along with the SQLAlchemy `Mapper` object (which defines the correlation of `class` attributes to database columns), Connection object that was/will be used to execute the query, and target object instance that was being acted on.

Generally, the idea is that the developer would use the raw connection object to execute simple SQL statements (for example, increment a counter, add a row to a logging table, and so on). We, however, will use the `after_insert` event to publish a summary of our recipe to both Twitter and Facebook.

To make things a bit simpler from an organizational standpoint, let's move the Twitter and Facebook OAuth client object instantiations to their own module in `application/users/services.py`:

```
from application import oauth

twitter = oauth.remote_app(
    'twitter',
    consumer_key='<consumer key>',
    consumer_secret='<consumer secret>',
    base_url='https://api.twitter.com/1/',
    request_token_url='https://api.twitter.com/oauth/request_token',
    access_token_url='https://api.twitter.com/oauth/access_token',
    authorize_url='https://api.twitter.com/oauth/authenticate',
    access_token_method='GET')
```

```
facebook = oauth.remote_app(
    'facebook',
    consumer_key='<consumer key>',
    consumer_secret='<consumer secret>',
    request_token_params={'scope': 'email,publish_actions'},
    base_url='https://graph.facebook.com',
    request_token_url=None,
    access_token_url='/oauth/access_token',
    access_token_method='GET',
    authorize_url='https://www.facebook.com/dialog/oauth')
```

In moving this functionality to a separate module, we can avoid some of the more nasty possibilities for circular imports. Now, in the `application/recipes/models.py` module, we will add the following function that will be invoked when the `after_insert` event is emitted and identified by the `listens_for` decorator:

```
from application.users.services import twitter, facebook
from sqlalchemy import event

@event.listens_for(Recipe, 'after_insert')
def listen_for_recipe_insert(mapper, connection, target):
    """Listens for after_insert event from SQLAlchemy
    for Recipe model instances."""

    summary = target.summarize()

    if target.user.twitter:
        twitter_response = twitter.post(
            'statuses/update.json',
            data={'status': summary})
        if twitter_response.status != 200:
            raise ValueError("Could not publish to Twitter.")

    if target.user.facebook:
        fb_response = facebook.post('/me/feed', data={
            'message': summary
        })
        if fb_response.status != 200:
            raise ValueError("Could not publish to Facebook.")
```

Our listener function only requires a target (the recipe instance that was acted on) for our purposes. We get the recipe summary thanks to our previously written `Recipe.summarize()` method, and then use the post method of both OAuth client objects (accounting for the different endpoint URIs and expected payload formats for each service) to create a status update across whichever services the user who posted the recipe has connected to.

> The error-handling code for the function that we defined here is somewhat inefficient; each API may return different HTTP error codes, and it's quite possible that one service may accept the post while the other would refuse it for some as yet unknown reason. Handling the various failure modes that may arise when interacting with multiple remote third-party APIs is complex and could be the subject of a book itself.

Finding common friends

A very typical feature of most modern, socially-oriented web applications is the ability to find users on an application that you are already familiar with on some other application social network. This helps you to bootstrap any sort of friendship/ follower model that you may want to implement for your application. Nobody likes to have zero friends on a new platform, so why not connect with the friends that you've already made in other places?

This is relatively easy to accomplish by finding the intersection of accounts that the user is following on Twitter and users that currently exist in the Dinnerly application.

> An intersection C of two sets, A and B, is the set of common elements that exist in A and B and no other elements.
>
> If you don't already understand the basic concepts of mathematical sets and the operations that can be performed on them, a primer on the naïve set theory should be on your reading list.

We start by adding a route handler that an authenticated user can query to find their list of common friends in our `application/users.views.py` module:

```
from flask import abort, render_template
from flask.ext.login import login_required

# …

@users.route('/twitter/find-friends')
@login_required
def twitter_find_friends():
```

```python
"""Find common friends."""

if not current_user.twitter:
    abort(403)

twitter_user_id = current_user.twitter.twitter_user_id

# This will only query 5000 Twitter user IDs.
# If your users have more friends than that,
# you will need to handle the returned cursor
# values to iterate over all of them.
response = twitter.get(
    'friends/ids?user_id={}'.format(twitter_user_id))

friends = response.json().get('ids', list())
friends = [int(f) for f in friends]

common_friends = User.query.filter(
    User.twitter_user_id.in_(friends))

return render_template('users/friends.html',
    friends=common_friends)
```

We used simple `abort()` calls in the preceding method, but there's nothing stopping you from creating templates that are rendered with additional information to help the end user understand why a certain operation failed.

The preceding view function is wrapped with the `login_required` decorator from our trusty Flask-Login extension to ensure that any request to this route is made by an authenticated user. An unauthenticated user would not be able to find common friends on Dinnerly for somewhat obvious reasons.

We then ensure that the authenticated user has connected a set of Twitter OAuth credentials and pluck out the `twitter_user_id` value so that we can properly construct the Twitter API request, which requires either the ID or `screen_name` of the user in question.

While `screen_name` might seem slightly easier to debug and reason about than a long numeric identifier, remember that it is possible for a person to update `screen_name` on Twitter at any time. If you wanted to rely on this value, you would need to write some code to verify and update the locally stored `screen_name` value if and when it does change on the remote service.

Once the GET request is made for the Twitter IDs of the people that the account follows on the remote service, we parse this result and construct a list of integers that we can then pass to a SQLAlchemy query on the User-mapped class. Now that we've obtained a list of users, we can pass these to our view (which we will not provide an implementation of – this is left as an exercise for the reader).

Of course, finding common friends is only half of the equation. Once we've found users that are our friends on Twitter, the next step is to follow them on Dinnerly as well. For this, we need to add a (minimal!) social component to our application, similar to what we implemented in a previous chapter.

This will require adding a few database-related entities, which we can do using our normal procedure of updating/adding the relevant models and then recreating the database schema, but we'll take this opportunity to explore a more formalized method of tracking schema-related changes.

Interlude – database migrations

For quite some time in the world of application development, we used a variety of tools to track and record code-related changes over time. Generally, these fall under the umbrella of version control systems, or VCS, and there are many of them to choose from: Git, Mercurial, Subversion, Perforce, Darcs, and several others. Each system functions in a slightly (or not so slightly) different manner, but they all have the same goal of preserving point-in-time snapshots of a codebase (or portions of a codebase, depending on the tool being used) so that it can be recreated at a later time.

One aspect of web applications that is generally difficult to capture and track is the current state of the database. In the past, we made do by storing entire SQL snapshots along with the application code and would instruct developers to drop and recreate their database. The next level of improvement on this would be the creation of small SQL-based scripts that should be run in a particular order to gradually build up the underlying schema progressively in such a way that when modifications are required, another small SQL-based script is added to the list.

While this latter method is quite flexible (it can work for almost any type of application that depends on a relational database), a slight abstraction that could leverage the functionality of the SQLAlchemy object-relational model that we already use would be beneficial.

Alembic

Such an abstraction already exists, and it's called Alembic. This library, by the same author of SQLAlchemy, allows us to create and manage the changesets that correspond to the schema modifications that are required to accommodate the modifications that are made to our SQLAlchemy data models.

As with most of the libraries that we've discussed over the course of this book, it has been wrapped in a Flask extension as Flask-Alembic. Let's install it in our current virtual environment:

```
$ pip install flask-alembic
```

As most of Flask-Alembic's functionalities can and should be controlled via CLI scripts, the package includes hooks to enable a Flask-Script command. So let's install this as well:

```
$ pip install flask-script
```

We will create our `manage.py` Python script to control our CLI commands as sibling to our `application/` package and ensure that it includes the db hooks to integrate Flask-Alembic:

```python
from flask.ext.script import Manager, Shell, Server
from application import create_app, db
from flask_alembic.cli.script import manager as alembic_manager


# Create the `manager` object with a
# callable that returns a Flask application object.
manager = Manager(app=create_app)


def _context():
    """Adds additional objects to our default shell context."""
    return dict(db=db)

if __name__ == '__main__':
    manager.add_command('db', alembic_manager)
    manager.add_command('runserver', Server(port=6000))
    manager.add_command('shell', Shell(make_context=_context))
    manager.run()
```

Now that we have both of these extensions installed, we need to configure the Flask-Alembic extension so that it's aware of our application object. We will do this in the usual way in our application factory function:

```python
# ...
from flask.ext.alembic import Alembic

# ...
# Intialize the Alembic extension
alembic = Alembic()


def create_app(config=None):
    app = Flask(__name__, static_folder=None)

    if config is not None:
        app.config.from_object(config)

    import application.users.models
    import application.recipes.models
        # ...
        alembic.init_app(app)

    from application.users.views import users
    app.register_blueprint(users, url_prefix='/users')

    return app
```

Let's capture the current database schema that is described by the SQLAlchemy models that we defined in our application:

```
$ python manage.py db revision 'Initial schema.'
```

This will create two new files in the `migrations/ folder` (which was created the first time this command was run), one of which will be named with a bunch of random characters followed by `_initial_schema.py`.

The random-looking characters are actually not so random: they are hash-based identifiers that help the migration system behave in a more predictable manner when there can be multiple developers working on migrations for different portions of the application all at the same time, which is somewhat typical these days.

The other file, `script.py.mako`, is the template that Alembic will utilize to generate these automatic revision summaries when the command is invoked. This script can be edited to suit your needs, but don't remove any of the template (`${foo}`) variables!

The generated migration file includes two function definitions: `upgrade()` and `downgrade()`. The upgrade function is run when Alembic takes the current database revision (which is `None` at this point) and attempts to bring it to the target (often the latest) revision. The `downgrade()` function does the same but for the opposite direction. Having both is very convenient for rollback-type situations, when switching between code branches that contain different sets of migrations, and several other edge cases. Many developers ignore the generation and testing of downgrade migrations and then sorely regret it at a later date in the lifetime of the project.

Your exact migration may look a little bit different based on what relational database you're using, but it should look something similar to this:

```python
"""Initial schema.

Revision ID: cd5ee4319a3
Revises:
Create Date: 2015-10-30 23:54:00.990549

"""

# revision identifiers, used by Alembic.
revision = 'cd5ee4319a3'
down_revision = None
branch_labels = ('default',)
depends_on = None

from alembic import op
import sqlalchemy as sa


def upgrade():
```

```
### commands auto generated by Alembic - please adjust! ###
op.create_table('user',
sa.Column('id', sa.Integer(), nullable=False),
sa.Column('username', sa.String(length=40), nullable=True),
sa.Column('created_on', sa.DateTime(), nullable=True),
sa.PrimaryKeyConstraint('id')
)
op.create_table('facebook_connection',
sa.Column('id', sa.Integer(), nullable=False),
sa.Column('user_id', sa.Integer(), nullable=False),
sa.Column('facebook_id', sa.Integer(), nullable=False),
sa.Column('access_token', sa.String(), nullable=False),
sa.Column('name', sa.String(), nullable=True),
sa.ForeignKeyConstraint(['user_id'], ['user.id'], ),
sa.PrimaryKeyConstraint('id'),
sa.UniqueConstraint('user_id')
)
op.create_table('recipe',
sa.Column('id', sa.Integer(), nullable=False),
sa.Column('title', sa.String(), nullable=True),
sa.Column('ingredients', sa.Text(), nullable=True),
sa.Column('instructions', sa.Text(), nullable=True),
sa.Column('created_on', sa.DateTime(), nullable=True),
sa.Column('user_id', sa.Integer(), nullable=True),
sa.ForeignKeyConstraint(['user_id'], ['user.id'], ),
sa.PrimaryKeyConstraint('id')
)
op.create_index(
    op.f('ix_recipe_created_on'), 'recipe',
    ['created_on'], unique=False)
op.create_table('twitter_connection',
sa.Column('id', sa.Integer(), nullable=False),
sa.Column('user_id', sa.Integer(), nullable=False),
sa.Column('screen_name', sa.String(), nullable=False),
sa.Column('twitter_user_id', sa.Integer(), nullable=False),
sa.Column('oauth_token', sa.String(), nullable=False),
sa.Column('oauth_token_secret', sa.String(), nullable=False),
sa.ForeignKeyConstraint(['user_id'], ['user.id'], ),
sa.PrimaryKeyConstraint('id'),
sa.UniqueConstraint('user_id')
)
### end Alembic commands ###
```

```
def downgrade():
    ### commands auto generated by Alembic - please adjust! ###
    op.drop_table('twitter_connection')
    op.drop_index(
        op.f('ix_recipe_created_on'), table_name='recipe')
    op.drop_table('recipe')
    op.drop_table('facebook_connection')
    op.drop_table('user')
    ### end Alembic commands ###
```

Now, there's quite a lot going on in this script, or at least it seems so. What's happening in the `upgrade()` function is the creation of the tables that correspond to the model metadata that we've defined in the application and the fields that belong to them. Alembic was able to infer what needed to be generated by comparing the current model definitions with the currently active database schema and outputting the list of commands that are required to synchronize them.

Most of the syntax elements should be relatively self-explanatory if you are familiar with relational database terminology (columns, primary keys, constraints, and so on), and you can read about what they all mean in the Alembic operation reference: `http://alembic.readthedocs.org/en/latest/ops.html`

With the initial schema migration generated, now it's time to apply it:

```
$ python manage.py db upgrade
```

This will emit the necessary SQL (based on the generated migration) to the RDBMS that you configured in the Flask-SQLAlchemy configuration.

Summary

After this rather lengthy and content-filled chapter, you should feel more at ease with OAuth and OAuth-related implementations and general terminology, and additionally, the usefulness of database migrations, especially the style of migrations produced by Alembic that are synchronized to the table and the constraint metadata declared in the application models.

The chapter started out with an in-depth exploration of the OAuth authorization grant flow and terminology—no small feat considering the complex nature of OAuth! Once we established a bit of a knowledge baseline, we implemented an application that leveraged Flask-OAuthlib to provide users with the ability to create accounts and sign in with third-party services such as Twitter and Facebook.

After fleshing out the data handling portions of the example application, we then turned our attention to Alembic, the SQLAlchemy data migration toolkit, to synchronize the changes in our models with our relational database.

The project that we started in this final chapter is a great kick-off point for most socially-aware web applications. You are highly encouraged to use the knowledge gained in this and the previous chapters to create a modern, highly-tested, functional web application.

Index

Thank you for buying
Flask Blueprints

About Packt Publishing

Packt, pronounced 'packed', published its first book, *Mastering phpMyAdmin for Effective MySQL Management*, in April 2004, and subsequently continued to specialize in publishing highly focused books on specific technologies and solutions.

Our books and publications share the experiences of your fellow IT professionals in adapting and customizing today's systems, applications, and frameworks. Our solution-based books give you the knowledge and power to customize the software and technologies you're using to get the job done. Packt books are more specific and less general than the IT books you have seen in the past. Our unique business model allows us to bring you more focused information, giving you more of what you need to know, and less of what you don't.

Packt is a modern yet unique publishing company that focuses on producing quality, cutting-edge books for communities of developers, administrators, and newbies alike. For more information, please visit our website at www.packtpub.com.

About Packt Open Source

In 2010, Packt launched two new brands, Packt Open Source and Packt Enterprise, in order to continue its focus on specialization. This book is part of the Packt Open Source brand, home to books published on software built around open source licenses, and offering information to anybody from advanced developers to budding web designers. The Open Source brand also runs Packt's Open Source Royalty Scheme, by which Packt gives a royalty to each open source project about whose software a book is sold.

Writing for Packt

We welcome all inquiries from people who are interested in authoring. Book proposals should be sent to author@packtpub.com. If your book idea is still at an early stage and you would like to discuss it first before writing a formal book proposal, then please contact us; one of our commissioning editors will get in touch with you.

We're not just looking for published authors; if you have strong technical skills but no writing experience, our experienced editors can help you develop a writing career, or simply get some additional reward for your expertise.

Web Development with Django Cookbook

ISBN: 978-1-78328-689-8   Paperback: 294 pages

Over 70 practical recipes to create multilingual, responsive, and scalable websites with Django

1. Improve your skills by developing models, forms, views, and templates.

2. Create a rich user experience using Ajax and other JavaScript techniques.

3. A practical guide to writing and using APIs to import or export data.

Flask Framework Cookbook

ISBN: 978-1-78398-340-7   Paperback: 258 pages

Over 80 hands-on recipes to help you create small-to-large web applications using Flask

1. Get the most out of the powerful Flask framework while remaining flexible with your design choices.

2. Build end-to-end web applications, right from their installation to the post-deployment stages.

3. Packed with recipes containing lots of sample applications to help you understand the intricacies of the code.

Rapid Flask
Gareth Dwyer

Rapid Flask [Video]

ISBN: 978-1-78355-425-6   Duration: 00:42 hrs

Get your web applications up and running in no time with Flask

1. Build a web app using Flask from beginning to end – never touch PHP again!

2. Not just "hello, world"- create a fully functional web app that includes web services, HTML forms, and more.

3. Your apps won't look like they came out of the '90s – learn how to integrate basic styles and icons.

4. Go further – Get a glimpse of how to utilize Flask's more popular extensions.

Flask Web Development
Tap into Flask to build a complete application in a style that you control
Ron DuPlain

Instant Flask Web Development

ISBN: 978-1-78216-962-8   Paperback: 78 pages

Tap into Flask to build a complete application in a style that you control

1. Learn something new in an Instant! A short, fast, focused guide delivering immediate results.

2. Build a small but complete web application with Python and Flask.

3. Explore the basics of web page layout using Twitter Bootstrap and jQuery.

4. Get to know how to validate data entry using HTML forms and WTForms.

Please check **www.PacktPub.com** for information on our titles